Quick & Easy
Chocolate

p

Contents

Introduction 4
Chocolate & Walnut Cake 6
Dark & White Chocolate Torte 7
Raspberry Vacherin 8
Chocolate Almond Cake 9
Chocolate Tea Bread 10
Bistvitny Torte 11
Chocolate & Orange Cake 12
Bûche de Noël 13
Apricot & Chocolate Ring 14
Chocolate Yogurt Cake 15
Family Chocolate Cake 16
Dobos Torte 17
Mocha Layer Cake 18
Chocolate Lamington Cake 19
Chocolate Truffle Cake 20
Chocolate Ganache Cake 21
Chocolate Passion Cake 22
Chocolate Roulade 23
Chocolate Layer Log 24
Rich Chocolate Layer Cake 25
Chocolate & Mango Layer 26
Devil's Food Cake 27
Chocolate Fudge Brownies 28
Chocolate Pretzels 29
Chocolate Butterfly Cakes 30
Chocolate Chip Flapjacks 31
Chocolate Boxes 32
Viennese Chocolate Fingers 33
Pain au Chocolate 34
Chocolate Eclairs 35
Chocolate Rum Babas 36
Malted Chocolate Wedges 37
Dutch Macaroons 38

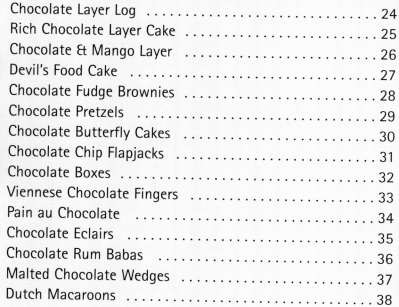

Chocolate Caramel Squares 39
Chocolate Chip Muffins 40
Chocolate Crispy Bites 41
No-Bake Chocolate Squares 42
Chocolate Scones 43
Pecan & Fudge Ring 44
Chocolate Apple Pie 45
Chocolate Fudge Pudding 46
Chocolate Queen of Puddings 47
Chocolate Fondue 48
Hot Chocolate Soufflé 49
Chocolate & Ginger Puddings 50
Bread & Butter Pudding 51
Chocolate & Banana Pancakes 52
Chocolate Meringue Pie 53
Chocolate Cheesecake 54
Marble Cheesecake 55
Chocolate Mint Swirls 56
Mississippi Mud Pie 57
Champagne Mousse 58
Chocolate Rum Pots 59
Chocolate Fruit Tartlets 60
Chocolate & Vanilla Creams 61
Profiteroles & Banana Cream 62
Chocolate Marquise 63
Tiramisu Layers 64
Iced White Chocolate Terrine 65
Chocolate Charlotte 66
Chocolate Banana Sundae 67
Black Forest Trifle 68
Banana–Coconut Cheesecake 69
Rich Chocolate Ice Cream 70
Easy Chocolate Fudge 71
Chocolate Liqueurs 72
Rocky Road Bites 73
Mini Chocolate Cones 74
Rum Truffles 75
Chocolate Marzipans 76
Chocolate & Mascarpone Cups 77
Hot Chocolate Drinks 78
Fruit & Nut Chocolate Fudge 79

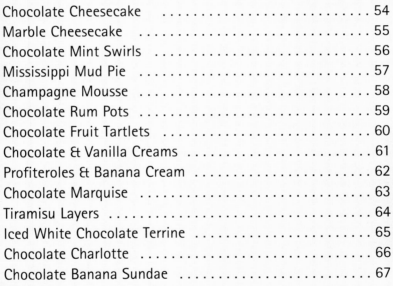

Introduction

Combining your favourite, most chocolatey dishes with some exciting new ideas for those who like to experiment, this fantastic collection contains recipes that are simple and fun to make at home. From familiar favourites, such as Black Forest Trifle, Butterfly Cakes and Chocolate Fudge Brownies, to more sumptuous dishes, such as rich Chocolate Fondue, tasty Truffles and the deliciously naughty Devil's Food Cake, this beautiful new book has them all. Some of these delicious recipes may need a little while to chill, set or freeze but they are quickly prepared and are well worth the wait! With recipes that cover all methods of cooking with chocolate, you will be able to indulge yourself no matter what you are craving: biscuits to be eaten at elevenses, profiteroles at lunch, rich chocolate cakes at tea, and sumptuous hot drinks to end an evening. Irresistible to most, these recipes are a must for chocoholics!

The History of Chocolate

With the discovery of the New World in the sixteenth century came the introduction of chocolate to the West. The Spanish first came across chocolate in the form of a highly spiced beverage, drunk by the Aztecs in

Mexico. When exported to Europe, it was treated as a prized possession and consumed by Spanish high society. Spreading throughout the continent, by the eighteenth century chocolate was believed to be a panacea. Confectioners became apothecaries promising to cure a variety of ills, from coughs and indigestion to inflammation and spasms. Today the genuine medicinal benefits of chocolate are doubtful but demand for this luxury has never been greater!

What is Chocolate?

Chocolate is produced from the beans of the cacao tree which are found within large pods. Once harvested,

both the pulp from the pods and the beans are fermented in the sun to develop the chocolatey flavour. The outer skin is then removed and the beans are left in the sun for a while longer or roasted. Finally, they are shelled and the kernels are used for making cocoa and chocolate.

Once ground and processed, the kernels produce 'cocoa solids'; from this we gauge the quality of the chocolate. The cocoa solids are then pressed to remove some of the fat — 'cocoa butter'. They are then further processed to produce the product that we know and love as chocolate.

The Quality of Chocolate

The quality of chocolate depends primarily on two things: the quality of the raw materials and the care taken at the different stages of manufacture — roasting and crushing the cocoa beans and mixing the cocoa paste or 'mass' with sugar and milk.

Good chocolate should have a shiny brown surface, break cleanly, and have no lumps, burst bubbles or white specks. It should melt on the tongue like butter, smell like chocolate rather than cocoa powder and be neither greasy or sticky.

The higher the percentage of cocoa solids, the softer the chocolate. Chocolate with a low amount of cocoa solids will be hard and brittle. Also, the more bitter the product, the more real chocolate flavour it has.

Storing Chocolate

Chocolate should be stored in a cool, dry place at about 18°C (64°F), away from direct sunlight or heat. Chocolate that does not contain milk can be kept for about a year. It can be stored in the refrigerator, but make sure it is well wrapped as it will pick up flavours from other foods. Keep chocolate decorations in an airtight container between non-stick baking parchment.

Melting Chocolate

Chocolate should not be melted over direct heat, except when melted with other ingredients, in which case the heat should be kept low. For the best results, break the chocolate into small, equally sized pieces and place them in a heatproof bowl. Place the bowl over a pan of hot water, making sure the base is not in contact with the water. Once the chocolate starts to melt, stir gently and if necessary leave over the water until all the chocolate is soft. Prevent any drops of water or steam from coming into contact with the melted chocolate as it will solidify.

To melt chocolate in the microwave, break the chocolate into small pieces and place in a microwave-proof bowl. As a guide, melt 125 g/4 $\frac{1}{2}$ oz dark chocolate on HIGH for 2 minutes and white or milk chocolate for 2–3 minutes on MEDIUM. Stir the chocolate and leave to stand for a few minutes, then stir again. Return to the microwave for a further 30 seconds if necessary. These times will vary according to the type of microwave and quality of chocolate used.

Types of Chocolate

Dark Chocolate: Mostly used in cooking, dark chocolate contains from 30 to 75 per cent cocoa solids and has a slightly bitter flavour and very dark colour. Choose a dark chocolate which has around 50 per cent cocoa solids; the higher the percentage the more intense the flavour. The best dark chocolate, also known as luxury or continental chocolate, has a cocoa solid content of between 70 and 75 per cent.

Milk Chocolate: Containing milk, this chocolate has a sweet, creamy flavour and is mostly used as an eating chocolate. It can be used in cooking when a milder flavour is required and for making decorations. However, it is more sensitive to heat than dark chocolate.

White Chocolate: This has a lower cocoa butter and cocoa solid content than milk chocolate. It is temperamental when heated so always choose a luxury white chocolate for cooking, taking care not to overheat it. White chocolate is useful for colour contrast especially in decorating.

Couverture: Although this retains a high gloss after melting and cooling, this is usually only used by professionals as it requires tempering. The recipes in this book do not included it as an ingredient.

Chocolate-Flavoured Cake Covering: The high fat content and low cocoa solid percentage makes this an unpopular chocolate with true chocolate lovers. Chocolate-flavoured cake covering can be added to dark chocolate to facilitate making cake decorations.

Chocolate Chips: These are excellent for baking and decorating and come in milk, white and dark chocolate flavours.

Cocoa Powder: This is the powder left after the cocoa butter has been pressed from the roasted and ground beans. It is unsweetened and bitter, giving a good, strong chocolate flavour when used in cooking.

Chocolate & Walnut Cake

This walnut-studded chocolate cake has a tasty chocolate butter icing.
It is perfect for coffee mornings as it can easily be made the day before.

NUTRITIONAL INFORMATION

Calories	517	Sugars	49g
Protein	8g	Fat	28g
Carbohydrate	61g	Saturates	14g

25 MINS   35 MINS

SERVES 8

INGREDIENTS

4 eggs

125 g/4½ oz/½ cup caster (superfine) sugar

125 g/4½ oz/1 cup plain (all-purpose) flour

1 tbsp cocoa powder

25 g/1 oz/2 tbsp butter, melted

75 g/2¾ oz dark chocolate, melted

150 g/5½ oz/1¼ cups finely chopped walnuts

ICING

75 g/2¾ oz dark chocolate

125 g/4½ oz/½ cup butter

200 g/7 oz/1¼ cups icing (confectioners') sugar

2 tbsp milk

walnut halves, to decorate

1 Grease a 18 cm/7 inch deep round cake tin (pan) and line the base. Place the eggs and caster (superfine) sugar in a mixing bowl and whisk with electric beaters for 10 minutes, or until the mixture is light and foamy and the whisk leaves a trail that lasts a few seconds when lifted.

2 Sieve (strain) together the flour and cocoa powder and fold in with a metal spoon or spatula. Fold in the melted butter and chocolate, and the chopped walnuts. Pour into the prepared tin (pan) and bake in a preheated oven, 160°C/325°F/Gas Mark 3, and bake for 30–35 minutes or until springy to the touch.

3 Leave to cool in the tin (pan) for 5 minutes, then transfer to a wire rack to cool completely. Cut the cold cake into 2 layers.

4 To make the icing, melt the dark chocolate and leave to cool slightly.

Beat together the butter, icing (confectioners') sugar and milk in a bowl until the mixture is pale and fluffy. Whisk in the melted chocolate.

5 Sandwich the 2 cake layers with some of the icing and place on a serving plate. Spread the remaining icing over the top of the cake with a palette knife (spatula), swirling it slightly as you do so. Decorate the cake with the walnut halves and serve.

Dark & White Chocolate Torte

If you can't decide if you prefer bitter dark chocolate or rich creamy white chocolate then this gateau is for you.

NUTRITIONAL INFORMATION

Calories 402	Sugars 30g
Protein 6g	Fat 26g
Carbohydrate . . . 38g	Saturates 15g

🍰 25 MINS   🕐 45 MINS

SERVES 10

I N G R E D I E N T S

4 eggs

100 g/3½ oz/7 tbsp cup caster (superfine) sugar

100 g/3½ oz/¾ cup plain (all-purpose) flour

DARK CHOCOLATE CREAM

300 ml/½ pint/⅔ cup double (heavy) cream

150 g/5½ oz dark chocolate, broken into small pieces

WHITE CHOCOLATE ICING

75 g/2¾ oz white chocolate

15 g/½ oz/1 tbsp butter

1 tbsp milk

50 g/1¾ oz/4 tbsp icing (confectioners') sugar

chocolate caraque

1 Grease a 20 cm/8 inch round springform tin (pan) and line the base. Whisk the eggs and caster (superfine) sugar in a large mixing bowl with electric beaters for about 10 minutes, or until the mixture is very light and foamy and the whisk leaves a trail that lasts a few seconds when lifted.

2 Sieve (strain) the flour and fold in with a metal spoon or spatula. Pour into the prepared tin (pan) and bake in a preheated oven, 180°C/350°F/Gas Mark 4, for 35–40 minutes, or until springy to the touch. Leave to cool slightly, then transfer to a wire rack to cool completely. Cut the cold cake into 2 layers.

3 To make the chocolate cream, place the cream in a saucepan and bring to the boil, stirring. Add the chocolate and stir until melted and well combined. Remove from the heat and leave to cool. Beat with a wooden spoon until thick.

4 Sandwich the 3 cake layers back together with the chocolate cream and place on a wire rack.

5 To make the icing, melt the chocolate and butter together and stir until blended. Whisk in the milk and icing (confectioners') sugar. Whisk for a few minutes until the icing is cool. Pour it over the cake and spread with a palette knife (spatula) to coat the top and sides. Decorate with chocolate caraque and leave to set.

COOK'S TIP

To make chocolate caraque, spread melted dark chocolate on a marble or acrylic board. As it begins to set, pull a knife through the chocolate at a 45° angle, working quickly to produce long, thin tubes of chocolate.

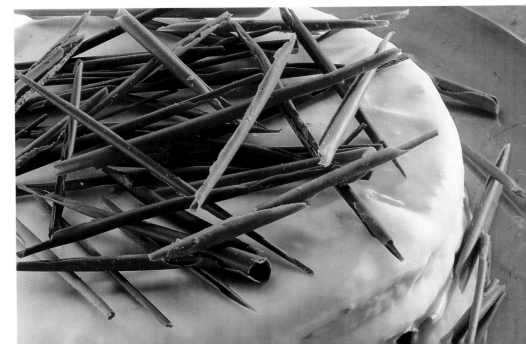

Raspberry Vacherin

A vacherin is made of layers of crisp meringue sandwiched together with fruit and cream. It makes a fabulous gateau for special occasions.

NUTRITIONAL INFORMATION

Calories 401	Sugars 35g
Protein 3g	Fat 28g
Carbohydrate . . . 36g	Saturates 17g

 30 MINS   1¹/₂ HRS

SERVES 10

I N G R E D I E N T S

3 egg whites

175 g/6 oz/¾ cup caster (superfine) sugar

1 tsp cornflour (cornstarch)

25 g/1 oz dark chocolate, grated

F I L L I N G

175 g/6 oz dark chocolate

450 ml/16 fl oz/2 cups double (heavy) cream, whipped

350 g/12 oz fresh raspberries

a little melted chocolate, to decorate

1 Draw 3 rectangles, 10 × 25 cm/ 4 × 10 inches, on sheets of baking parchment and place on 2 baking trays (cookie sheets).

2 Whisk the egg whites in a mixing bowl until standing in soft peaks, then gradually whisk in half of the sugar and continue whisking until the mixture is very stiff and glossy.

3 Carefully fold in the rest of the sugar, the cornflour (cornstarch) and grated chocolate with a metal spoon or a spatula.

4 Spoon the meringue mixture into a piping bag fitted with a 1 cm/¹/₂ inch plain nozzle (tip) and pipe lines across the rectangles.

5 Bake in a preheated oven, 140°C/275°F/Gas Mark 1, for 1¹/₂ hours, changing the positions of the baking trays (cookie sheets) halfway through. Without opening the oven door, turn off the oven and leave the meringues to cool in the oven, then peel away the paper.

6 To make the filling, melt the chocolate and spread it over 2 of the meringue layers. Leave the filling to harden.

7 Place 1 chocolate-coated meringue on a plate and top with about one-third of the cream and raspberries. Gently place the second chocolate-coated meringue on top and spread with half of the remaining cream and raspberries.

8 Place the last meringue on the top and decorate it with the remaining cream and raspberries. Drizzle a little melted chocolate over the top and serve.

Chocolate Almond Cake

Chocolate and almonds complement each other perfectly in this delicious cake. Be warned, one slice will never be enough!

NUTRITIONAL INFORMATION

Calories 702	Sugars 42g	
Protein 11g	Fat 53g	
Carbohydrate . . . 48g	Saturates 27g	

   50 MINS   45 MINS

SERVES 8

I N G R E D I E N T S

175 g/6 oz dark chocolate

175 g/6 oz/¾ cup butter

125 g/4½ oz caster (superfine) sugar

4 eggs, separated

¼ tsp cream of tartar

50 g/1¾ oz/⅓ cup self-raising flour

125 g/4½ oz/1¼ cups ground almonds

1 tsp almond flavouring (extract)

T O P P I N G

125 g/4½ oz milk chocolate

25 g/1 oz/2 tbsp butter

4 tbsp double (heavy) cream

T O   D E C O R A T E

25 g/1 oz/2 tbsp toasted flaked almonds

25 g/1 oz dark chocolate, melted

1 Lightly grease and line the base of a 23 cm/9 inch round springform tin (pan). Break the chocolate into small pieces and place in a small pan with the butter. Heat gently, stirring until melted and well combined.

2 Place 100 g/3½ oz/7 tbsp of the caster (superfine) sugar in a bowl with the egg yolks and whisk until pale and creamy. Add the melted chocolate mixture, beating until well combined.

3 Sieve (strain) the cream of tartar and flour together and fold into the chocolate mixture with the ground almonds and almond flavouring (extract).

4 Whisk the egg whites in a bowl until standing in soft peaks. Add the remaining caster (superfine) sugar and whisk for about 2 minutes by hand, or 45–60 seconds, if using an electric whisk, until thick and glossy. Fold the egg whites into the chocolate mixture and spoon into the tin (pan). Bake in a preheated oven, 190°C/375°F/Gas Mark 5, for 40 minutes until just springy to the touch. Let cool.

5 Heat the topping ingredients in a bowl over a pan of hot water. Remove from the heat and beat for 2 minutes. Let chill for 30 minutes. Transfer the cake to a plate and spread with the topping. Scatter with the almonds and drizzle with melted chocolate. Leave to set for 2 hours before serving.

Chocolate Tea Bread

What better in the afternoon than to sit down with a cup of tea and a slice of tea bread, and when it's made of chocolate it's even better.

NUTRITIONAL INFORMATION

Calories 452	Sugars 32g	
Protein 7g	Fat 27g	
Carbohydrate . . . 49g	Saturates 14g	

 15 MINS   1 HR 10 MINS

SERVES 10

I N G R E D I E N T S

175 g/6 oz/¾ cup butter, softened

100 g/3½ oz light muscovado sugar

4 eggs, lightly beaten

225 g/8 oz dark chocolate chips

100 g/3½ oz/½ cup raisins

50 g/1¾ oz/½ cup chopped walnuts finely grated rind of 1 orange

225 g/8 oz/2 cups self-raising flour

3 Gradually add the eggs, beating well after each addition. If the mixture begins to curdle, beat in 1–2 tablespoons of the flour.

4 Stir in the chocolate chips, raisins, walnuts and orange rind. Sieve (strain) the flour and carefully fold it into the mixture.

5 Spoon the mixture into the prepared loaf tin (pan) and make a slight dip in the centre of the top with the back of a spoon.

6 Bake in a preheated oven, 170°C/325°F/Gas Mark 3, for 1 hour or until a fine skewer inserted into the centre of the loaf comes out clean.

7 Leave to cool in the tin (pan) for 5 minutes, before carefully turning out and leaving on a wire rack to cool completely.

8 Serve the tea bread cut into thin slices.

1 Lightly grease a 900 g/2 lb loaf tin (pan) and line the base with baking parchment.

2 Cream together the butter and sugar in a bowl until light and fluffy.

VARIATION

Use white or milk chocolate chips instead of dark chocolate chips, or a mixture of all three, if desired. Dried cranberries instead of the raisins also work well in this recipe.

Bistvitny Torte

This is a Russian marbled chocolate cake that is soaked in a delicious flavoured syrup and decorated with chocolate and cream.

NUTRITIONAL INFORMATION

Calories	478	Sugars	38g
Protein	5g	Fat	27g
Carbohydrate	55g	Saturates	10g

25 MINS | 40 MINS

SERVES 10

INGREDIENTS

CHOCOLATE TRIANGLES

25 g/1 oz dark chocolate, melted

25 g/1 oz white chocolate, melted

CAKE

175 g/6 oz/¾ cup soft margarine 175 g/6 oz/¾ cup caster (superfine) sugar

½ tsp vanilla flavouring (extract)

3 eggs, lightly beaten

225 g/8 oz/2 cups self-raising flour

50 g/1¾ oz dark chocolate

SYRUP

125 g/4½ oz/½ cup sugar

6 tbsp water

3 tbsp brandy or sherry

150 ml/¼ pint/⅔ cup double (heavy) cream

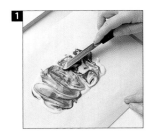

1 Grease a 23 cm/9 inch ring tin (pan). To make the triangles, place a sheet of baking parchment on to a baking tray (cookie sheet) and place alternate spoonfuls of the dark and white chocolate on to the paper. Spread together to form a thick marbled layer; leave to set. Cut into squares, then into triangles.

2 To make the cake, beat the margarine and sugar until light and fluffy. Beat in the vanilla flavouring (extract). Gradually add the eggs, beating well after each addition. Fold in the flour. Divide the mixture in half. Melt the dark chocolate and stir into one half.

3 Place spoonfuls of each mixture into the prepared tin (pan) and swirl together with a skewer to create a marbled effect.

4 Bake in a preheated oven, 190°C/ 375°F/Gas Mark 5, for 30 minutes, or until the cake is springy to the touch. Leave to cool in the tin (pan) for a few minutes, then transfer to a wire rack to cool completely.

5 To make the syrup, place the sugar in a small pan with the water and heat until the sugar has dissolved. Boil for 1–2 minutes. Remove from the heat and stir in the brandy or sherry. Leave the syrup to cool slightly then spoon it slowly over the cake, allowing it to soak into the sponge. Whip the cream and pipe swirls of it on top of the cake. Decorate with the chocolate triangles.

Chocolate & Orange Cake

A popular combination of flavours, this cake is ideal for a tea-time treat.
Omit the icing, if preferred, and sprinkle with icing (confectioners') sugar.

NUTRITIONAL INFORMATION

Calories	 455	Sugars	.... 47g
Protein	.... 6g	Fat	.... 21g
Carbohydrate	... 64g	Saturates	..... 13g

20 MINS   25 MINS

SERVES 8

I N G R E D I E N T S

175 g/6 oz/¾ cup caster (superfine) sugar

175 g/6 oz/¾ cup butter or block margarine

3 eggs, beaten

175 g/6 oz/1½ cups self-raising flour, sieved (strained)

2 tbsp cocoa powder, sieved (strained)

2 tbsp milk

3 tbsp orange juice

grated rind of ½ orange

I C I N G

175 g/6 oz/1 cup icing (confectioners') sugar

2 tbsp orange juice

1 Lightly grease a 20 cm/8 inch deep round cake tin (pan).

2 Beat together the sugar and butter or margarine in a bowl until light and fluffy. Gradually add the eggs, beating well after each addition. Carefully fold in the flour.

3 Divide the mixture in half. Add the cocoa powder and milk to one half, stirring until well combined. Flavour the other half with the orange juice and rind.

4 Place spoonfuls of each mixture into the prepared tin (pan) and swirl together with a skewer, to create a marbled effect. Bake in a preheated oven,

190°C/375°F/Gas Mark 5, for 25 minutes or until springy to the touch.

5 Leave the cake to cool in the tin (pan) for a few minutes before transferring to a wire rack to cool completely.

6 To make the icing, sift the icing (confectioners') sugar into a mixing bowl and mix in enough of the orange juice to form a smooth icing. Spread the icing over the top of the cake and leave to set before serving.

VARIATION

Add 2 tablespoons of rum or brandy to the chocolate mixture instead of the milk. The cake also works well when flavoured with grated lemon rind and juice instead of the orange.

Bûche de Noël

This is the traditional French Christmas cake. It consists of a chocolate Swiss roll filled and encased in a delicious rich chocolate icing.

NUTRITIONAL INFORMATION

Calories 397	Sugars 31g	
Protein 7g	Fat 24g	
Carbohydrate . . . 39g	Saturates 14g	

20 MINS   25 MINS

SERVES 8

I N G R E D I E N T S

CAKE

4 eggs

100 g/3½ oz/7 tbsp caster (superfine) sugar

75 g/2¾ oz/⅔ cup self-raising flour

2 tbsp cocoa powder

ICING

150 g/5½ oz dark chocolate

2 egg yolks

150 ml/¼ pint/⅔ cup milk

125 g/4½ oz/½ cup butter

50 g/1¾ oz/4 tbsp icing (confectioners') sugar

2 tbsp rum (optional)

TO DECORATE

a little white glacé or royal icing

icing (confectioners') sugar, to dust

holly or Christmas cake decorations

1 Grease and line a 30 × 23 cm/12 × 9 inch Swiss roll tin (pan). Whisk the eggs and caster (superfine) sugar in a bowl with electric beaters for 10 minutes, or until the mixture is very light and foamy and the whisk leaves a trail. Sieve (strain) the flour and cocoa powder and fold in. Pour into the prepared tin (pan) and bake in a preheated oven, 200°C/400°F/Gas Mark 6, for 12 minutes or until springy to the touch. Turn out on to a piece of baking parchment which has been sprinkled with a little caster (superfine) sugar. Peel off the lining paper and trim the edges. Cut a small slit halfway into the cake about 1 cm/½ inch from one short end. Starting at that end, roll up tightly, enclosing the paper. Place on a wire rack to cool.

2 To make the icing, break the chocolate into pieces and melt it over a pan of hot water. Beat in the egg yolks, whisk in the milk and cook until the mixture thickens enough to coat the back of a wooden spoon, stirring. Cover with dampened greaseproof paper and cool. Beat the butter and sugar until pale and fluffy. Beat in the custard and rum, if using. Unroll the sponge, spread with one-third of the icing and roll up again. Place on a serving plate. Spread the remaining icing over the cake and mark with a fork to give the effect of bark. Leave to set. Pipe white icing to form the rings of the log. Sprinkle with sugar and decorate.

Apricot & Chocolate Ring

A tasty tea bread in the shape of a ring. You could use sultanas instead of the apricots, if preferred.

NUTRITIONAL INFORMATION

Calories 296	Sugars 17g	
Protein 6g	Fat 17g	
Carbohydrate ... 45g	Saturates 12g	

 15 MINS   35 MINS

SERVES 12

INGREDIENTS

75 g/2¾ oz/⅓ cup butter, diced

450 g/1 lb/4 cups self-raising flour, sieved (strained)

50 g/1¾ oz/4 tbsp caster (superfine) sugar

2 eggs, beaten

150 ml/¼ pint/⅔ cup milk

FILLING AND DECORATION

25 g/1 oz/2 tbsp butter, melted

150 g/5½ oz ready-to-eat dried apricots, chopped

100 g/3½ oz dark chocolate chips

1–2 tbsp milk, to glaze

25 g/1 oz dark chocolate, melted

1 Grease a 25 cm/10 inch round cake tin (pan) and line the base with baking parchment.

2 Rub the butter into the flour until the mixture resembles fine breadcrumbs. Stir in the caster (superfine) sugar, eggs and milk to form a soft dough.

3 Roll out the dough on a lightly floured surface to form a 35 cm/14 inch square.

4 Brush the melted butter over the surface of the dough. Mix together the apricots and chocolate chips and spread them over the dough to within 2.5 cm/1 inch of the top and bottom.

5 Roll up the dough tightly, like a Swiss roll, and cut it into 2.5 cm/1 inch slices. Stand the slices in a ring around the edge of the prepared tin (pan) at a slight tilt. Brush with a little milk.

6 Bake in a preheated oven, 180°C/350°F/Gas Mark 4, for 30 minutes or until cooked and golden. Leave to cool in the tin (pan) for about 15 minutes, then transfer to a wire rack to cool.

7 Drizzle the melted chocolate over the ring, to decorate.

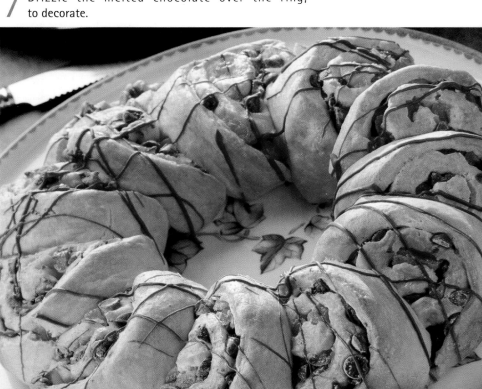

COOK'S TIP

This cake is best served very fresh, ideally on the day it is made. It is fabulous served slightly warm.

Chocolate Yogurt Cake

The yogurt added to the cake mixture gives the baked cake a deliciously moist texture.

NUTRITIONAL INFORMATION

Calories 537   Sugars 32g
Protein . . . . 10g   Fat 34g
Carbohydrate . . . 57g   Saturates 11g

🍰 25 MINS   🕐 45 MINS

SERVES 8

I N G R E D I E N T S

150 ml/¼ pint/⅔ cup vegetable oil

150 ml/¼ pint/⅔ cup whole milk natural yogurt

175 g/6 oz/1¼ cups light muscovado sugar

3 eggs, beaten

100 g/3½ oz/¾ cup wholemeal (whole wheat) self-raising flour

125 g/4½ oz/1 cup self-raising flour, sieved (strained)

2 tbsp cocoa powder

1 tsp bicarbonate of soda (baking soda)

50 g/1¾ oz dark chocolate, melted

150 ml/¼ pint/⅔ cup whole milk natural yogurt

150 ml/¼ pint/⅔ cup double (heavy) cream

225 g/8 oz fresh soft fruit, such as strawberries or raspberries

1 Grease a deep 23 cm/9 inch round cake tin (pan) and line the base with baking parchment .

2 Place the oil, yogurt, sugar and beaten eggs in a large mixing bowl and beat together until well combined. Sieve (strain) the flours, cocoa powder and bicarbonate of soda (baking soda) together and beat into the bowl until well combined. Beat in the melted chocolate.

3 Pour into the prepared tin (pan) and bake in a preheated oven, 180°C/350°F/Gas Mark 4, for 45–50 minutes or until a fine skewer inserted into the centre comes out clean. Leave to cool in the tin (pan) for 5 minutes, then turn out on to a wire rack to cool completely. When cold, split the cake into 3 layers.

4 Place the yogurt and cream in a large mixing bowl and whisk well until the mixture stands in soft peaks.

5 Place one layer of cake on to a serving plate and spread with some of the cream. Top with a little of the fruit (slicing larger fruit such as strawberries). Repeat with the next layer. Top with the final layer of cake and spread with the rest of the cream. Arrange more fruit on top and cut the cake into wedges to serve.

Family Chocolate Cake

A simple to make family cake ideal for an everyday treat. Keep the decoration as simple as you like – you could use a bought icing or filling.

NUTRITIONAL INFORMATION

Calories 384   Sugars 32g
Protein . . . . 5g   Fat 22g
Carbohydrate . . . 44g   Saturates 8g

 20 MINS   25 MINS

SERVES 8

INGREDIENTS

125 g/4½ oz/½ cup soft margarine

125 g/4½ oz/½ cup caster (superfine) sugar

2 eggs

1 tbsp golden (light corn) syrup

125 g/4½ oz/1 cup self-raising flour, sieved (strained)

2 tbsp cocoa powder, sieved (strained)

FILLING AND TOPPING

50 g/1¾ oz/¼ cup icing (confectioners') sugar, sieved (strained)

25 g/1 oz/2 tbsp butter

100 g/3½ oz white or milk cooking chocolate

a little milk or white chocolate, melted (optional)

COOK'S TIP

Ensure that you eat this cake on the day of baking, as it does not keep well.

1 Lightly grease two 18 cm/7 inch shallow cake tins (pans).

2 Place all of the ingredients for the cake in a large mixing bowl and beat with a wooden spoon or electric hand whisk to form a smooth mixture.

3 Divide the mixture between the prepared tins (pans) and level the tops. Bake in a preheated oven, 190°C/325F/Gas Mark 5, for 20 minutes or until springy to the touch. Cool for a few minutes in the tins (pans) before transferring to a wire rack to cool completely.

4 To make the filling, beat the icing (confectioners') sugar and butter together in a bowl until light and fluffy. Melt the cooking chocolate and beat half into the icing mixture. Use the filling to sandwich the 2 cakes together.

5 Spread the remaining melted cooking chocolate over the top of the cake. Pipe circles of contrasting melted milk or white chocolate and feather into the cooking chocolate with a cocktail stick (toothpick), if liked. Leave to set before serving.

Dobos Torte

This wonderful sponge cake originates from Hungary. It is sandwiched together with butter cream and topped with a crunchy caramel layer.

NUTRITIONAL INFORMATION

Calories	621	Sugars	16g
Protein	5g	Fat	27g
Carbohydrate	96g	Saturates	16g

25 MINS 15 MINS

SERVES 8

INGREDIENTS

3 eggs

100 g/3½ oz/7 tbsp caster (superfine) sugar

1 tsp vanilla flavouring (extract)

100 g/3½ oz/½ cup plain (all-purpose) flour

FILLING

175 g/6 oz dark chocolate

175 g/6 oz/¾ cup butter

2 tbsp milk

350 g/12 oz/2 cups icing (confectioners') sugar

CARAMEL

100 g/3½ oz/7 tbsp granulated sugar

4 tbsp water

  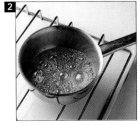

1 Draw four 18 cm/7 inch circles on sheets of baking parchment. Place 2 of them upside down on 2 baking trays (cookie sheets). Whisk the eggs and caster (superfine) sugar in a large mixing bowl with electric beaters for 10 minutes, or until the mixture is light and foamy and the whisk leaves a trail. Fold in the vanilla flavouring (extract). Sieve (strain) the flour and fold in with a metal spoon or a spatula. Spoon a quarter of the mixture on to one of the trays (sheets) and spread out to the size of the circle.

Repeat with the other circle. Bake in a preheated oven, 200°C/400°F/Gas Mark 6, for 5–8 minutes or until golden brown. Cool on wire racks. Repeat with the remaining mixture.

2 To make the filling, melt the chocolate and cool slightly. Beat the butter, milk and icing (confectioners') sugar until pale and fluffy. Whisk in the chocolate. Place the sugar and water for the caramel in a heavy-based pan and heat gently, stirring until the sugar

dissolves. Boil gently until the syrup is pale golden. Remove from the heat. Pour over one layer of the cake to cover the top. Leave to harden slightly, then mark into 8 portions with an oiled knife. Remove the cakes from the paper and trim the edges. Sandwich the layers together with some of the filling, finishing with the caramel-topped cake. Place on a serving plate and spread the sides with the filling mixture, using a comb scraper if you have one. Pipe rosettes around the top of the cake.

Mocha Layer Cake

Chocolate cake and a creamy coffee-flavoured filling are combined in this delicious mocha cake.

NUTRITIONAL INFORMATION

Calories 588   Sugars 26g
Protein . . . . 8g   Fat 43g
Carbohydrate . . . 46g   Saturates 17g

25 MINS   40 MINS

SERVES 8

INGREDIENTS

200 g/7¾ oz/1 cups self-raising flour

¼ tsp baking powder

4 tbsp cocoa powder

100 g/3½ oz/7 tbsp caster (superfine) sugar

2 eggs

2 tbsp golden (light corn) syrup

150 ml/¼ pint/⅔ cup sunflower oil

150 ml/¼ pint/⅔ cup milk

FILLING

1 tsp instant coffee

1 tbsp boiling water

300 ml/½ pint/1¼ cups double (heavy) cream

25 g/1 oz/2 tbsp icing (confectioners') sugar

TO DECORATE

50 g/1¾ oz flock chocolate

chocolate caraque (see page 7)

icing (confectioners') sugar, to dust

1 Lightly grease three 18 cm/7 inch cake tins (pans).

2 Sieve (strain) the flour, baking powder and cocoa powder into a large mixing bowl. Stir in the sugar. Make a well in the centre and stir in the eggs, syrup, oil and milk. Beat with a wooden spoon, gradually mixing in the dry ingredients to make a smooth batter. Divide the mixture between the prepared tins (pans).

3 Bake in a preheated oven, 180°C/350°F/Gas Mark 4, for 35–45 minutes or until springy to the touch. Leave in the tins (pans) for 5 minutes, then turn out on to a wire rack to cool completely.

4 Dissolve the instant coffee in the boiling water and place in a bowl with the cream and icing (confectioners') sugar.

Whip until the cream is just holding it's shape. Use half of the cream to sandwich the 3 cakes together. Spread the remaining cream over the top and sides of the cake. Lightly press the flock chocolate into the cream around the edge of the cake.

5 Transfer to a serving plate. Lay the caraque over the top of the cake. Cut a few thin strips of baking parchment and place on top of the caraque. Dust lightly with icing (confectioners') sugar, then carefully remove the paper. Serve.

Chocolate Lamington Cake

This chocolate and coconut cake is based on the Australian Lamington cake, named after Lord Lamington, a former Governor of Queensland.

NUTRITIONAL INFORMATION

Calories 581	Sugars 45g	
Protein 7g	Fat 37g	
Carbohydrate ...59g	Saturates 24g	

25 MINS   45 MINS

SERVES 8

INGREDIENTS

175 g/6 oz/¾ cup butter or block margarine

175 g/6 oz/¾ cup caster (superfine) sugar

3 eggs, lightly beaten

150 g/5½ oz/1¼ cups self-raising flour

2 tbsp cocoa powder

125 g/4½ oz/¾ cup icing (confectioners') sugar

50 g/1¾ oz dark chocolate, broken into pieces

5 tbsp milk

1 tsp butter

about 8 tbsp desiccated (shredded) coconut

150 ml/¼ pint double (heavy) cream, whipped

1 Lightly grease a 450 g/1 lb loaf tin (pan) – preferably a long, thin tin (pan) about 7.5 × 25 cm/3 × 10 inches.

2 Cream together the butter and sugar in a bowl until light and fluffy. Gradually add the eggs, beating well after each addition. Sieve (strain) together the flour and cocoa. Fold into the mixture.

3 Pour the mixture into the prepared tin (pan) and level the top. Bake in a preheated oven, 180°C/350°F/Gas Mark 4, for 40 minutes or until springy to the touch. Leave to cool for 5 minutes in the tin (pan), then turn out on to a wire rack to cool completely.

4 Place the chocolate, milk and butter in a heatproof bowl set over a pan of hot water. Stir until the chocolate has melted. Add the icing (confectioners') sugar and beat until smooth. Leave to cool until the icing is thick enough to spread, then spread it all over the cake.

Sprinkle with the desiccated (shredded) coconut and allow the icing to set.

5 Cut a V-shape wedge from the top of the cake. Put the cream in a piping bag fitted with a plain or star nozzle (tip). Pipe the cream down the centre of the wedge and replace the wedge of cake on top of the cream. Pipe another line of cream down either side of the wedge of cake. Serve.

Chocolate Truffle Cake

Soft chocolatey sponge topped with a rich chocolate truffle mixture makes a cake that chocoholics will die for.

NUTRITIONAL INFORMATION

Calories 520	Sugars 31g
Protein 6g	Fat 39g
Carbohydrate . . . 37g	Saturates 22g

4 HOURS   35 MINS

SERVES 12

I N G R E D I E N T S

75 g/2¾ oz/⅓ cup butter

75 g/2¾ oz/⅓ cup caster (superfine) sugar

2 eggs, lightly beaten

75 g/2¾ oz/⅔ cup self-raising flour

½ tsp baking powder

25 g/1 oz/¼ cup cocoa powder

50 g/1¾ oz ground almonds

T R U F F L E   T O P P I N G

350 g/12 oz dark chocolate

100 g/3½ oz butter

300 ml/½ pint/1¼ cups double (heavy) cream

75 g/2¾ oz/1¼ cups plain cake crumbs

3 tbsp dark rum

T O   D E C O R A T E

Cape gooseberries (ground cherries)

50 g/1¾ oz dark chocolate, melted

1 Lightly grease a 20 cm/8 inch round springform tin (pan) and line the base. Beat together the butter and sugar until light and fluffy. Gradually add the eggs, beating well after each addition.

2 Sieve (strain) the flour, baking powder and cocoa powder together and fold into the mixture along with the ground almonds. Pour into the prepared tin (pan) and bake in a preheated oven, 180°C/350°F/Gas Mark 4, for 20–25 minutes or until springy to the touch. Leave to cool slightly in the tin (pan), then transfer to a wire rack to cool completely. Wash and dry the tin (pan) and return the cooled cake to the tin (pan).

3 To make the topping, heat the chocolate, butter and cream in a heavy-based pan over a low heat and stir until smooth. Cool, then chill for 30 minutes. Beat well with a wooden spoon and chill for a further 30 minutes. Beat the mixture again, then add the cake crumbs and rum, beating until well combined. Spoon over the sponge base and chill for 3 hours.

4 Meanwhile, dip the Cape gooseberries (ground cherries) in the melted chocolate until partially covered. Leave to set on baking parchment. Transfer the cake to a serving plate; decorate with Cape gooseberries (ground cherries).

Chocolate Ganache Cake

Ganache – a divine mixture of chocolate and cream – is used to fill and decorate this rich chocolate cake, making it a chocolate lover's dream.

NUTRITIONAL INFORMATION

Calories 809	Sugars 55g	
Protein 9g	Fat 57g	
Carbohydrate . . . 70g	Saturates 36g	

🍰 1 HR 25 MINS   🕐 45 MINS

SERVES 10

I N G R E D I E N T S

175 g/6 oz/¾ cup butter

175 g/6 oz/¾ cup caster (superfine) sugar

4 eggs, lightly beaten

200 g/7 oz/1¾ cups self-raising flour

1 tbsp cocoa powder

50 g/1¾ oz dark chocolate, melted

G A N A C H E

450ml/16 fl oz/2 cups double (heavy) cream

375 g/13 oz dark chocolate, broken into pieces

T O   F I N I S H

200 g/7 oz chocolate-flavoured cake covering

1 Lightly grease a 20 cm/8 inch springform cake tin (pan) and line the base. Beat the butter and sugar until light and fluffy. Gradually add the eggs, beating well after each addition. Sieve (strain) together the flour and cocoa. Fold into the cake mixture. Fold in the melted chocolate.

2 Pour into the prepared tin (pan) and level the top. Bake in a preheated oven, 180°C/350°F/Gas Mark 4, for 40 minutes or until springy to the touch. Leave to cool for 5 minutes in the tin (pan), then turn out on to a wire rack and leave to cool completely . Cut the cold cake into 2 layers.

3 To make the ganache, place the cream in a pan and bring to the boil, stirring. Add the chocolate and stir until melted and combined. Pour into a bowl and whisk for about 5 minutes or until the ganache is fluffy and cool.

4 Reserve one-third of the ganache. Use the remaining ganache to sandwich the cake together and spread over the top and sides of the cake.

5 Melt the cake covering and spread it over a large sheet of baking parchment. Cool until just set. Cut into strips a little wider than the height of the cake. Place the strips around the edge of the cake, overlapping them slightly.

6 Pipe the reserved ganache in tear drop or shells to cover the top of the cake. Chill for 1 hour.

Chocolate Passion Cake

What could be nicer than passion cake with added chocolate?
Rich and moist, this cake is fabulous with afternoon tea.

NUTRITIONAL INFORMATION

Calories 436   Sugars 47g
Protein . . . . 11g   Fat 19g
Carbohydrate . . . 60g   Saturates 7g

20 MINS   50 MINS

SERVES 10

INGREDIENTS

5 eggs

150 g/5½ oz/⅔ cup caster (superfine) sugar

150 g/5½ oz/1¼ cups plain (all-purpose) flour

40 g/1½ oz/⅓ cup cocoa powder

175 g/6 oz carrots, peeled and finely grated

50 g/1¾ oz/½ cup chopped walnuts

2 tbsp sunflower oil

350 g/12 oz medium fat soft cheese

175 g/6 oz/1 cup icing (confectioners') sugar

175 g/6 oz milk or dark chocolate, melted

1 Lightly grease and line the base of a 20 cm/8 inch deep round cake tin (pan).

2 Place the eggs and sugar in a large mixing bowl set over a pan of gently simmering water and whisk until very thick. Lift the whisk up and let the mixture drizzle back – it will leave a trail for a few seconds when thick enough.

3 Remove the bowl from the heat. Sieve (strain) the flour and cocoa powder into the bowl and carefully fold in. Fold in the carrots, walnuts and oil until just combined.

4 Pour into the prepared tin (pan) and bake in a preheated oven, 190°C/375°F/Gas Mark 5, for 45 minutes or until well risen and springy to the touch. Leave to cool slightly then turn out on to a wire rack to cool completely.

5 Beat together the soft cheese and icing (confectioners') sugar until combined. Beat in the melted chocolate. Split the cake in half and sandwich together again with half of the chocolate mixture. Cover the top of the cake with the remainder of the chocolate mixture, swirling it with a knife. Leave to chill or serve at once.

COOK'S TIP

The undecorated cake can be frozen for up to 2 months. Defrost at room temperature for 3 hours or overnight in the refrigerator.

Chocolate Roulade

Don't worry if the cake cracks when rolled, this is normal. If it doesn't crack, you can consider yourself a real wizard in the kitchen!

NUTRITIONAL INFORMATION

Calories	584	Sugars	48g
Protein	11g	Fat	38g
Carbohydrate	52g	Saturates	21g

25 MINS   15 MINS

SERVES 6

I N G R E D I E N T S

150 g/5½ oz dark chocolate

2 tbsp water

6 eggs

175 g/6 oz/¾ cup caster (superfine) sugar

25 g/1 oz/¼ cup plain (all-purpose) flour

1 tbsp cocoa powder

F I L L I N G

300 ml/½ pint/1¼ cups double (heavy) cream)

75 g/2¾ oz sliced strawberries

T O   D E C O R A T E

icing (confectioners') sugar

chocolate leaves (see step 5)

1 Line a 37.5 × 25 cm/15 × 10 inch Swiss roll tin (pan). Melt the chocolate in the water, stirring. Leave to cool slightly.

2 Place the eggs and sugar in a bowl and whisk for 10 minutes, or until the mixture is pale and foamy and the whisk leaves a trail when lifted. Whisk in the chocolate in a thin stream. Sieve (strain) the flour and cocoa together and fold into the mixture. Pour into the tin; level the top.

3 Bake in a preheated oven, 200°C/400°F/Gas Mark 6, for 12 minutes. Dust a sheet of baking parchment with a little icing (confectioners') sugar. Turn out the roulade and remove the lining paper. Roll up the roulade with the fresh parchment inside. Place on a wire rack, cover with a damp tea towel and leave to cool.

4 Whisk the cream until just holding its shape. Unroll the roulade and scatter over the fruit. Spread three-quarters of the cream over the roulade and re-roll. Dust with icing (confectioners') sugar. Place the roulade on a plate. Pipe the rest of the cream down the centre and decorate with chocolate leaves.

5 To make chocolate leaves, wash some rose or holly leaves and pat dry. Melt some chocolate and brush over the leaves. Set aside to harden. Repeat with 2–3 layers of chocolate. Carefully peel the leaves away from the chocolate.

Chocolate Layer Log

This unusual cake is very popular with children who love the appearance of the layers when it is sliced.

NUTRITIONAL INFORMATION

Calories 514	Sugars 40g
Protein 5g	Fat 34g
Carbohydrate . . . 50g	Saturates 16g

20 MINS   45 MINS

SERVES 8

I N G R E D I E N T S

125 g/4½ oz/½ cup soft margarine

125 g/4½ oz/½ cup caster (superfine) sugar

2 eggs

100 g/3½ oz/¾ cup self-raising flour

25 g/1 oz/¼ cup cocoa powder

2 tbsp milk

WHITE CHOCOLATE BUTTER CREAM

75 g/2¾ oz white chocolate

2 tbsp milk

150 g/5½ oz/⅔ cup butter

125 g/4½ oz/¾ cup icing (confectioners') sugar

2 tbsp orange-flavoured liqueur

large dark chocolate curls (see page 57), to decorate

1 Grease and line the sides of two 400 g/14 oz food cans.

2 Beat together the margarine and sugar in a bowl until light and fluffy. Gradually add the eggs, beating well after each addition. Sieve (strain) together the flour and cocoa powder and fold into the cake mixture. Fold in the milk.

3 Divide the mixture between the two prepared cans. Stand the cans on a baking tray (cookie sheet) and bake in a preheated oven, 180°C/350°F/Gas Mark 4, for 40 minutes or until springy to the touch. Leave to cool for about 5 minutes in the cans, then turn out and leave to cool completely on a wire rack.

4 To make the butter cream, put the chocolate and milk in a pan and heat gently until the chocolate has melted, stirring until well combined. Leave to cool slightly. Beat together the butter and icing (confectioners') sugar until light and fluffy. Beat in the orange liqueur. Gradually beat in the chocolate mixture.

5 To assemble, cut both cakes into 1 cm/½ inch thick slices, then reassemble them by sandwiching the slices together with some of the butter cream.

6 Place the cake on a serving plate and spread the remaining butter cream over the top and sides. Decorate with the chocolate curls, then serve the cake cut diagonally into slices.

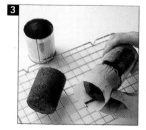

Rich Chocolate Layer Cake

Thin layers of delicious light chocolate cake sandwiched together with a rich chocolate icing.

NUTRITIONAL INFORMATION

Calories 505	Sugars 39g	
Protein 10g	Fat 30g	
Carbohydrate . . . 52g	Saturates 15g	

 25 MINS 35 MINS

SERVES 10

I N G R E D I E N T S

7 eggs

200 g/7 oz/1¾ cups caster (superfine) sugar

150 g/5½ oz/1¼ cups plain (all-purpose) flour

50 g/1¾ oz/½ cup cocoa powder

50 g/1¾ oz/4 tbsp butter, melted

F I L L I N G

200 g/7 oz dark chocolate

125 g/4½ oz/½ cup butter

50 g/1¾ oz/4 tbsp icing (confectioners') sugar

T O   D E C O R A T E

75 g/2¾ oz/10 tbsp toasted flaked almonds, crushed lightly

small chocolate curls (see page 57) or grated chocolate

1 Grease a deep 23 cm/9 inch square cake tin (pan) and line the base with baking parchment.

2 Whisk the eggs and caster (superfine) sugar in a mixing bowl with an electric whisk for about 10 minutes, or until the mixture is very light and foamy and the whisk leaves a trail that lasts a few seconds when lifted.

3 Sieve (strain) the flour and cocoa together and fold half into the mixture. Drizzle over the melted butter and fold in the rest of the flour and cocoa. Pour into the prepared tin (pan) and bake in a preheated oven, 180°C/350°F/ Gas Mark 4, for 30–35 minutes or until springy to the touch. Leave to cool slightly, then remove from the tin (pan) and cool completely on a wire rack. Wash and dry the tin (pan) and return the cake to it.

4 To make the filling, melt the chocolate and butter together, then remove from the heat. Stir in the icing (confectioners') sugar, leave to cool, then beat until thick enough to spread.

5 Halve the cake lengthways and cut each half into 3 layers. Sandwich the layers together with three-quarters of the chocolate filling. Spread the remainder over the cake and mark a wavy pattern on the top. Press the almonds on to the sides. Decorate with chocolate curls or grated chocolate.

Chocolate & Mango Layer

If the top of the cake is very domed, level off, then turn the cake upside down leaving a flat surface to decorate. Peaches can be used instead of mangoes.

NUTRITIONAL INFORMATION

Calories 491	Sugars 47g
Protein 8g	Fat 23g
Carbohydrate . . . 67g	Saturates 13g

25 MINS   1 HOUR 5 MINS

SERVES 12

I N G R E D I E N T S

50 g/1¾ oz/½ cup cocoa powder

150 ml/¼ pint/⅔ cup boiling water

6 large eggs

350 g/12 oz/1½ cups caster (superfine) sugar

300 g/10½ oz/2½ cups self-raising flour

2 x 400 g/14 oz cans mango

1 tsp cornflour (cornstarch)

425 ml/¾ pint/generous 1¾ cups double (heavy) cream

75 g/2¾ oz dark flock chocolate or grated chocolate

1 Grease a deep 23 cm/9 inch round cake tin (pan) and line the base with baking parchment.

2 Place the cocoa powder in a small bowl and gradually add the boiling water; blend to form a smooth paste.

3 Place the eggs and caster (superfine) sugar in a mixing bowl and whisk until the mixture is very light and foamy and the whisk leaves a trail that lasts a few seconds when lifted. Fold in the cocoa mixture. Sieve (strain) the flour and fold into the mixture.

4 Pour the mixture into the tin (pan) and level the top. Bake in a preheated oven, 170°C/325°F/ Gas Mark 3, for about 1 hour or until springy to the touch.

5 Leave to cool in the tin (pan) for a few minutes then turn out and cool completely on a wire rack. Peel off the lining paper and cut the cake into 3 layers.

6 Drain the mangoes and place a quarter of them in a food processor and purée until smooth. Mix the cornflour (cornstarch) with about 3 tbsp of the mango juice to form a smooth paste. Add to the mango purée. Transfer to a small pan and heat gently, stirring until the purée thickens. Leave to cool.

7 Chop the remaining mango. Whip the cream and reserve about one quarter. Fold the mango into the remaining cream and use to sandwich the layers of cake together. Place on a serving plate. Spread some of the remaining cream around the side of the cake. Press the flock or grated chocolate lightly into the cream. Pipe cream rosettes around the top. Spread the mango purée over the centre.

Devil's Food Cake

This is an American classic, consisting of a rich melt-in-the-mouth chocolate cake that has a citrus-flavoured frosting.

NUTRITIONAL INFORMATION

Calories 685	Sugars 99g
Protein 6g	Fat 29g
Carbohydrate . . 109g	Saturates 18g

🍰 25 MINS   🕐 35 MINS

SERVES 8

I N G R E D I E N T S

100 g/3½ oz dark chocolate

250 g/9 oz/2¼ cups self-raising flour

1 tsp bicarbonate of soda (baking soda)

225 g/8 oz/1 cup butter

400 g/14 oz/2⅔ cups dark muscovado sugar

1 tsp vanilla flavouring (extract)

3 eggs

125 ml/4 fl oz/½ cup buttermilk

225 ml/8 fl oz/2 cups boiling water

F R O S T I N G

300 g/10½ oz/1⅓ cups caster (superfine) sugar

2 egg whites

1 tbsp lemon juice

3 tbsp orange juice

candied orange peel, to decorate

1 Lightly grease two 20 cm/8 inch shallow round cake tins (pans) and line the bases. Melt the chocolate in a pan. Sieve (strain) the flour and bicarbonate of soda (baking soda) together.

2 Beat the butter and sugar in a bowl until pale and fluffy. Beat in the vanilla flavouring (extract) and the eggs, one at a time and beating well after each addition. Add a little flour if the mixture begins to curdle.

3 Fold the melted chocolate into the mixture until well blended. Gradually fold in the remaining flour, then stir in the buttermilk and boiling water.

4 Divide the mixture between the tins (pans) and level the tops. Bake in a preheated oven, 190°C/375°F/Gas Mark 5, for 30 minutes until springy to the touch. Leave to cool in the tin (pan) for 5 minutes, then transfer to a wire rack to cool completely.

5 Place the frosting ingredients in a large bowl set over a pan of gently simmering water. Whisk, preferably with an electric beater, until thickened and forming soft peaks. Remove from the heat and whisk until the mixture is cool.

6 Sandwich the 2 cakes together with a little of the frosting, then spread the remainder over the sides and top of the cake, swirling it as you do so. Decorate with the candied orange peel.

Chocolate Fudge Brownies

Here a traditional brownie mixture has a cream cheese ribbon through the centre and is topped with a delicious chocolate fudge icing.

NUTRITIONAL INFORMATION

Calories	193	Sugars	23g
Protein	5g	Fat	7g
Carbohydrate	29g	Saturates	3g

 25 MINS   45 MINS

MAKES 16

INGREDIENTS

200 g/7 oz low-fat soft cheese

½ tsp vanilla flavouring (extract)

2 eggs

250 g/9 oz/generous 1 cup caster (superfine) sugar

100 g/3½ oz/generous ⅓ cup butter

3 tbsp cocoa powder

100 g/3½ oz/¾ cup self-raising flour, sieved (strained)

50 g/1¾ oz pecans, chopped

FUDGE ICING

50 g/1¾ oz/1 tbsp butter

1 tbsp milk

100 g/3½ oz/½ cup icing (confectioners') sugar

2 tbsp cocoa powder

pecans, to decorate (optional)

VARIATION

Omit the cheese layer if preferred. Use walnuts in place of the pecans.

1 Lightly grease a 20 cm/8 inch square shallow cake tin (pan) and line the base.

2 Beat together the cheese, vanilla flavouring (extract) and 25 g/1 oz/5 tsp of the caster (superfine) sugar until smooth, then set aside.

3 Beat the eggs and remaining caster (superfine) sugar together until light and fluffy. Place the butter and cocoa powder in a small pan and heat gently, stirring until the butter melts and the mixture combines, then stir it into the egg mixture. Fold in the flour and nuts.

4 Pour half of the brownie mixture into the tin (pan) and level the top. Carefully spread the soft cheese over it, then cover it with the remaining brownie mixture. Bake in a preheated oven, 180°C/350°F/Gas Mark 4, for 40–45 minutes. Cool in the tin (pan).

5 To make the icing, melt the butter in the milk. Stir in the icing (confectioners') sugar and cocoa powder. Spread the icing over the brownies and decorate with pecan nuts, if using. Leave the icing to set, then cut into squares to serve.

Chocolate Pretzels

If you thought of pretzels as savouries, then think again. These are fun to make and prove that pretzels come in a sweet variety, too.

NUTRITIONAL INFORMATION

Calories	90	Sugars	6g
Protein	1g	Fat	5g
Carbohydrate	12g	Saturates	3g

40 MINS 12 MINS

MAKES 30

INGREDIENTS

100 g/3½ oz/generous ⅓ cup unsalted butter

100 g/3½ oz/7 tbsp caster (superfine) sugar

1 egg

225 g/8 oz/2 cups plain (all-purpose) flour

25 g/1 oz/¼ cup cocoa powder

TO FINISH

15 g/½ oz/1 tbsp butter

100 g/3½ oz dark chocolate

icing (confectioners') sugar, to dust

1 Lightly grease a baking tray (cookie sheet). Beat together the butter and sugar in a mixing bowl until light and fluffy. Beat in the egg.

2 Sift together the flour and cocoa powder and gradually beat in to form a soft dough. Use your fingers to incorporate the last of the flour and bring the dough together. Chill for 15 minutes.

3 Break pieces from the dough and roll into thin sausage shapes about 10 cm/4 inches long and 6 mm/¼ inch thick. Twist into pretzel shapes by making a circle, then twist the ends through each other to form a letter 'B'.

4 Place on the prepared baking tray (cookie sheet), slightly spaced apart to allow for spreading during cooking.

5 Bake in a preheated oven, 190°C/375°F/Gas Mark 5, for 8–12 minutes. Leave the pretzels to cool slightly on the baking tray (cookie sheet), then transfer to a wire rack to cool completely.

6 Melt the butter and chocolate in a bowl set over a pan of gently simmering water, stirring to combine.

7 Dip half of each pretzel into the chocolate and allow the excess chocolate to drip back into the bowl. Place the pretzels on a sheet of baking parchment and leave to set.

8 When set, dust the non-chocolate coated side of each pretzel with icing (confectioners') sugar before serving.

Chocolate Butterfly Cakes

Filled with a tangy lemon cream these appealing cakes will be a favourite with adults and children alike.

NUTRITIONAL INFORMATION

Calories 331	Sugars 32g	
Protein 3g	Fat 18g	
Carbohydrate ... 42g	Saturates 7g	

20 MINS   20 MINS

MAKES 12

I N G R E D I E N T S

125 g/4½ oz/½ cup soft margarine

125 g/4½ oz/½ cup caster (superfine) sugar

150 g/5½ oz/1¼ cups self-raising flour

2 large eggs

2 tbsp cocoa powder

25 g/1 oz dark chocolate, melted

L E M O N   B U T T E R   C R E A M

100 g/3½ oz/ generous ⅓ cup unsalted butter, softened

225 g/8 oz/1⅓ cups icing (confectioners') sugar, sieved (strained)

grated rind of ½ lemon

1 tbsp lemon juice

icing (confectioners') sugar, to dust

1 Place 12 paper cases in a bun tray (sheet). Place all of the ingredients for the cakes, except for the melted chocolate, in a large mixing bowl and beat with electric beaters until the mixture is just smooth. Beat in the chocolate.

2 Spoon equal amounts of the cake mixture into each paper case, filling them three-quarters full. Bake in a preheated oven, 180°C/350°F/Gas Mark 4, for 15 minutes or until springy to the touch. Transfer the cakes to a wire rack and leave to cool.

3 To make the lemon butter cream, place the butter in a mixing bowl and beat until fluffy, then gradually beat in the icing (confectioners') sugar. Beat in the lemon rind and gradually add the lemon juice, beating well.

4 When cold, cut the top off each cake, using a serrated knife. Cut each top in half.

5 Spread or pipe the butter cream icing over the cut surface of each cake and push the 2 cut pieces of cake top into the icing to form wings. Sprinkle with icing (confectioners') sugar.

VARIATION

For a chocolate butter cream, beat the butter and icing (confectioners') sugar together, then beat in 25 g/ 1 oz melted dark chocolate.

Chocolate Chip Flapjacks

Turn flapjacks into something special by adding chocolate chips. Dark chocolate is used here, but you can use milk or white chocolate instead.

NUTRITIONAL INFORMATION

Calories 267	Sugars 15g
Protein 4g	Fat 13g
Carbohydrate . . . 36g	Saturates 7g

 15 MINS   35 MINS

MAKES 12

I N G R E D I E N T S

125 g/4½ oz/½ cup butter

75 g/2¾ oz/⅓ cup caster (superfine) sugar

1 tbsp golden (light corn) syrup

350 g/12 oz/4 cups rolled oats

75 g/2¾ oz/½ cup dark chocolate chips

50 g/1¾ oz/⅓ cup sultanas (golden raisins)

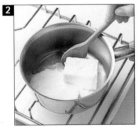

VARIATION

For a really special flapjack, replace some of the oats with chopped nuts or sunflower seeds and a little extra dried fruit.

1 Lightly grease a shallow 20 cm/8 inch square cake tin (pan).

2 Place the butter, caster (superfine) sugar and golden (light corn) syrup in a saucepan and cook over a low heat, stirring until the butter and sugar melt and the mixture is well combined.

3 Remove the pan from the heat and stir in the rolled oats until they are well coated. Add the chocolate chips and the sultanas (golden raisins) and mix well to combine everything.

4 Turn into the prepared tin (pan) and press down well.

5 Bake in a preheated oven, 180°C/350°F/Gas Mark 4, for 30 minutes. Cool slightly, then mark into fingers. When almost cold cut into bars or squares and transfer to a wire rack until cold.

Chocolate Boxes

People will think you have spent hours in the kitchen producing these, but with a few tricks you can make them in no time at all.

NUTRITIONAL INFORMATION

Calories	606	Sugars	63g
Protein	7g	Fat	32g
Carbohydrate	76g	Saturates	11g

 30 MINS   0 MINS

SERVES 4

I N G R E D I E N T S

225 g/8 oz dark chocolate

about 225 g/8 oz bought or ready-made plain or chocolate cake

2 tbsp apricot jam

150 ml/¼ pint/⅔ cup double (heavy) cream

1 tbsp maple syrup

100 g/3½ oz prepared fresh fruit, such as small strawberries, raspberries, kiwi fruit or redcurrants

1 Melt the dark chocolate and spread it evenly over a large sheet of baking parchment. Leave to harden in a cool room.

2 When just set, cut the chocolate into 5 cm/2 inch squares and remove from the paper. Make sure that your hands are as cool as possible and handle the chocolate as little as possible.

3 Cut the cake into two 5 cm/2 inch cubes, then each cube in half. Warm the apricot jam and brush it over the sides of the cake cubes. Carefully press a chocolate square on to each side of the cake cubes to give 4 chocolate boxes with cake at the bottom. Leave to chill for 20 minutes.

4 Whip the double (heavy) cream with the maple syrup until just holding its shape. Spoon or pipe a little of the mixture into each chocolate box.

5 Decorate the top of each box with the prepared fruit. If liked, the fruit can be partially dipped into melted chocolate and allowed to harden before putting into the boxes.

COOK'S TIP

For the best results, keep the boxes well chilled and fill and decorate them just before you want to serve them.

Viennese Chocolate Fingers

These biscuits (cookies) have a fabulously light, melting texture. You can leave them plain or dip them in chocolate to decorate.

NUTRITIONAL INFORMATION

Calories .... 161 Sugars 11g
Protein .... 1g Fat 9g
Carbohydrate ... 20g Saturates 6g

 20 MINS   15 MINS

MAKES 18

INGREDIENTS

125 g/4½ oz/½ cup unsalted butter

75 g/2¾ oz/6 tbsp icing (confectioners') sugar

175 g/6 oz/1½ cups self-raising flour, sieved (strained)

25 g/1 oz/3 tbsp cornflour (cornstarch)

200 g/7 oz dark chocolate

1 Lightly grease 2 baking trays (cookie sheets). Beat the butter and sugar in a mixing bowl until light and fluffy. Gradually beat in the flour and cornflour (cornstarch).

2 Melt 75 g/2¾ oz of the dark chocolate and beat into the biscuit dough.

3 Place in a piping bag fitted with a large star nozzle (tip) and pipe fingers about 5 cm/2 inches long on the baking trays (cookie sheets), slightly spaced apart to allow for spreading.

4 Bake in a preheated oven, 190°C/375°F/Gas Mark 5, for 12–15 minutes. Leave to cool slightly on the baking trays (cookie sheets), then transfer with a palette knife (spatula) to a wire rack and leave to cool completely.

5 Melt the remaining chocolate and dip one end of each biscuit (cookie) in the chocolate, allowing the excess to drip back into the bowl.

6 Place the biscuits (cookies) on a sheet of baking parchment and leave to set before serving.

VARIATION

Dip the base of each biscuit in melted chocolate and leave to set. Sandwich the biscuits (cookies) together in pairs with a little butter cream.

Pain au Chocolate

These can be a little fiddly to make, but when you taste the light pastry and fabulous filling you know they are worth it.

NUTRITIONAL INFORMATION

Calories 309	Sugars 6g
Protein 5g	Fat 18g
Carbohydrate ... 35g	Saturates 11g

1 HR 50 MINS · 25 MINS

MAKES 12

INGREDIENTS

450 g/1 lb/4 cups strong plain (all-purpose) flour

½ tsp salt

6 g sachet of easy blend yeast

25 g/1 oz/2 tbsp white vegetable fat

1 egg, beaten lightly

225 ml/8 fl oz/1 cup tepid water

175 g/6 oz/¾ cup butter, softened

100 g/3½ oz dark chocolate, broken into 12 squares

beaten egg, to glaze

icing (confectioners') sugar, to dust

3 Fold the rectangle into 3 by first folding the plain part of the dough over and then the other side. Seal the edges of the dough by pressing with a rolling pin. Give the dough a quarter turn so the sealed edges are at the top and bottom. Re-roll and fold (without adding butter), then wrap the dough and chill for 30 minutes.

4 Repeat steps 2 and 3 until all of the butter has been used, chilling the dough each time. Re-roll and fold twice more without butter. Chill for a final 30 minutes.

5 Roll the dough to a rectangle 45 × 30 cm/18 × 12 inches, trim and halve lengthways. Cut each half into 6 rectangles and brush with beaten egg. Place a chocolate square at one end of each rectangle and roll up to form a sausage. Press the ends together and place, seamside down, on the baking tray (cookie sheet). Cover and leave to rise for 40 minutes in a warm place. Brush with egg and bake in a preheated oven, 220°C/425°F/Gas Mark 7, for 20–25 minutes until golden. Cool on a wire rack. Serve warm or cold.

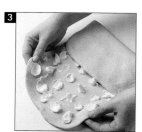

1 Lightly grease a baking tray (cookie sheet). Sieve (strain) the flour and salt into a mixing bowl and stir in the yeast. Rub in the fat with your fingertips. Add the egg and enough of the water to mix to a soft dough. Knead it for about 10 minutes to make a smooth elastic dough.

2 Roll out to form a rectangle 37.5 × 20 cm/15 × 8 inches. Divide the butter into 3 portions and dot one portion over two-thirds of the rectangle, leaving a small border around the edge.

Chocolate Eclairs

Patisserie cream is the traditional filling for éclairs, but if time is short you can fill them with whipped cream.

NUTRITIONAL INFORMATION

Calories	216	Sugars	16g
Protein	4g	Fat	10g
Carbohydrate	29g	Saturates	6g

 30 MINS   35 MINS

MAKES 10

INGREDIENTS

CHOUX PASTRY (PIE DOUGH)

150 ml/¼ pint/⅔ cup water

60 g/2 oz/¼ cup butter, cut into small pieces

90 g/3 oz/¾ cup strong plain (all-purpose) flour, sieved (strained)

2 eggs

PATISSERIE CREAM

2 eggs, lightly beaten

50 g/1¾ oz/4 tbsp caster (superfine) sugar

2 tbsp cornflour (cornstarch)

300 ml/½ pint/1¼ cups milk

¼ tsp vanilla flavouring (extract)

ICING

25 g/1 oz/2 tbsp butter

1 tbsp milk

1 tbsp cocoa powder

100 g/3½ oz/½ cup icing (confectioners') sugar

a little white chocolate, melted

 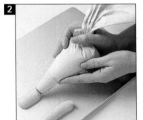 

1 Lightly grease a baking tray (cookie sheet). Place the water in a saucepan, add the butter and heat gently until the butter melts. Bring to a rolling boil, then remove the pan from the heat and add the flour in one go, beating well until the mixture leaves the sides of the pan and forms a ball. Leave to cool slightly, then gradually beat in the eggs to form a smooth, glossy mixture. Spoon into a large piping bag fitted with a 1 cm/½ inch plain nozzle (tip).

2 Sprinkle the tray (sheet) with a little water. Pipe éclairs 7.5 cm/ 3 inches long, spaced well apart. Bake in a preheated oven, 200°C/400°F/Gas Mark 6, for 30–35 minutes or until crisp and golden. Make a small slit in each one to let the steam escape; cool on a rack.

3 To make the patisserie cream, whisk the eggs and sugar until thick and creamy, then fold in the cornflour (cornstarch). Heat the milk until almost boiling and pour on to the eggs, whisking. Transfer to the pan and cook over a low heat, stirring until thick. Remove the pan from the heat and stir in the flavouring (extract). Cover with baking parchment and cool. To make the icing, melt the butter with the milk in a pan, remove from the heat and stir in the cocoa and sugar. Split the éclairs lengthways and pipe in the patisserie cream. Spread the icing over the top of the éclair. Spoon over the white chocolate, swirl in and leave to set.

Chocolate Rum Babas

A little fiddly but well worth the effort. Indulge in these tasty cakes with coffee or serve as a dessert with soft summer fruits.

NUTRITIONAL INFORMATION

Calories	 4	Sugars	.... 26g
Protein	.... 5g	Fat	.... 15g
Carbohydrate	... 46g	Saturates	...... 9g

  2 HRS 25 MINS   20 MINS

SERVES 4

I N G R E D I E N T S

100 g/3½ oz/¾ cup strong plain
   (all-purpose) flour

25 g/1 oz/¼ cup cocoa powder

6 g sachet easy blend yeast

pinch of salt

15 g/½ oz/1 tbsp caster (superfine) sugar

40 g/1½ oz dark chocolate, grated

2 eggs

3 tbsp tepid milk

50 g/1¾ oz/4 tbsp butter, melted

S Y R U P

4 tbsp clear honey

2 tbsp water

4 tbsp rum

T O   S E R V E

whipped cream

cocoa powder, to dust

fresh fruit (optional)

1 Lightly oil 4 individual ring tins (pans). In a large warmed mixing bowl, sieve (strain) the flour and cocoa powder together. Stir in the yeast, salt, sugar and grated chocolate. Beat the eggs together, add the milk and butter and beat until mixed.

2 Make a well in the centre of the dry ingredients and pour in the egg mixture, beating to mix to a batter. Beat for 10 minutes, ideally in a electric mixer with a dough hook. Divide the mixture between the tins (pans) – it should come halfway up the sides.

3 Place on a baking tray (cookie sheet) and cover with a damp tea towel.

Leave in a warm place until the mixture rises almost to the tops of the tins (pans). Bake in a preheated oven, 200°C/400°F/ Gas Mark 6, for 15 minutes.

4 To make the syrup, gently heat all of the ingredients in a small pan. Turn out the babas and place on rack placed above a tray to catch the syrup. Drizzle the syrup over the babas and leave for at least 2 hours for the syrup to soak in. Once or twice, spoon the syrup that has dripped on to the tray over the babas.

5 Fill the centre of the babas with whipped cream and sprinkle a little cocoa powder over the top. Serve the babas with fresh fruit, if desired.

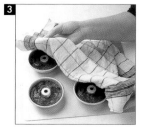

Malted Chocolate Wedges

These are perfect with a bedtime drink, although you can enjoy these tasty biscuit (cookie) wedges at any time of the day.

NUTRITIONAL INFORMATION

Calories 157	Sugars 11g
Protein 1g	Fat 9g
Carbohydrate . . . 19g	Saturates 5g

 15 MINS   0 MINS

MAKES 16

I N G R E D I E N T S

100 g/3½ oz/generous ⅓ cup butter

2 tbsp golden (light corn) syrup

2 tbsp malted chocolate drink

225 g/8 oz malted milk biscuits (cookies)

75 g/2¾ oz milk or dark chocolate, broken into pieces

25 g/1 oz/2 tbsp icing (confectioners') sugar

2 tbsp milk

1 Grease a shallow 18 cm/7 inch round cake tin (pan) or flan tin (pan) and line the base.

2 Place the butter, golden (light corn) syrup and malted chocolate drink in a small pan and heat gently, stirring all the time until the butter has melted and the mixture is well combined.

3 Crush the biscuits (cookies) in a plastic bag with a rolling pin, or process them in a food processor until they form crumbs. Stir the crumbs into the chocolate mixture and mix well.

4 Press the mixture into the prepared tin (pan) and chill in the refrigerator until firm.

5 Place the chocolate pieces in a small heatproof bowl with the icing (confectioners') sugar and the milk. Place the bowl over a pan of gently simmering water and stir until the chocolate melts and the mixture is combined.

6 Spread the chocolate icing over the biscuit (cookie) base and leave to set in the tin (pan). Using a sharp knife, cut into wedges to serve.

VARIATION

Add chopped pecan nuts to the biscuit (cookie) crumb mixture in step 3, if liked.

Dutch Macaroons

These unusual biscuit (cookie) treats are delicious served with coffee.
They also make an ideal dessert biscuit (cookie) to serve with ice cream.

NUTRITIONAL INFORMATION

Calories 150	Sugars 19g
Protein 3g	Fat 8g
Carbohydrate . . . 20g	Saturates 2g

 20 MINS   20 MINS

MAKES 20

I N G R E D I E N T S

rice paper

2 egg whites

225 g/8 oz/1 cup caster (superfine) sugar

175 g/6 oz/1⅓ cups ground almonds

225 g/8 oz dark chocolate

1 Cover 2 baking trays (cookie sheets) with rice paper. Whisk the egg whites in a large mixing bowl until stiff, then fold in the sugar and ground almonds.

2 Place the mixture in a large piping bag fitted with a 1 cm/½ inch plain nozzle (tip) and pipe fingers, about 7.5 cm/3 inches long, allowing space for the mixture to spread during cooking.

3 Bake in a preheated oven, 180°C/350°F/Gas Mark 4, for 15–20 minutes until golden. Transfer to a wire rack and leave to cool. Remove the excess rice paper from around the edges.

4 Melt the chocolate and dip the base of each biscuit into the chocolate. Place the macaroons on a sheet of baking parchment and leave to set.

5 Drizzle any remaining chocolate over the top of the biscuits (cookies). Leave to set before serving.

VARIATION

Almonds are most commonly used in macaroons, but they can be made with other ground nuts, such as hazelnuts.

Chocolate Caramel Squares

It is difficult to say 'No' to these biscuits (cookies), which consist of a crunchy base, a creamy caramel filling and a chocolate top.

NUTRITIONAL INFORMATION

Calories .... 163 Sugars 13g
Protein .... 2g Fat 9g
Carbohydrate ... 21g Saturates 3g

 25 MINS   30 MINS

MAKES 16

INGREDIENTS

100 g/3½ oz/generous ⅓ cup soft margarine
50 g/1¾ oz/4 tbsp light muscovado sugar
125 g/4½ oz/1 cup plain (all-purpose) flour
40 g/1½ oz/½ cup rolled oats

CARAMEL FILLING

25 g/1 oz/2 tbsp butter
25 g/1 oz/2 tbsp light muscovado sugar
200 g/7 oz can condensed milk

TOPPING

100 g/3½ oz dark chocolate
25 g/1 oz white chocolate (optional)

1 Beat together the margarine and muscovado sugar in a bowl until light and fluffy. Beat in the flour and the rolled oats. Use your fingertips to bring the mixture together, if necessary.

2 Press the mixture into the base of a shallow 20 cm/8 inch square cake tin (pan).

3 Bake in a preheated oven, 180°C/350°F/Gas Mark 4, for 25 minutes or until just golden and firm. Cool in the tin (pan).

4 Place the ingredients for the caramel filling in a pan and heat gently, stirring until the sugar has dissolved and the ingredients combine. Bring slowly to the boil over a very low heat, then boil very gently for 3–4 minutes, stirring constantly until thickened.

5 Pour the caramel filling over the biscuit base in the tin (pan) and leave to set.

6 Melt the dark chocolate and spread it over the caramel. If using the white chocolate, melt it and pipe lines of white chocolate over the dark chocolate. Using a cocktail stick (toothpick) or a skewer, feather the white chocolate into the dark chocolate. Leave to set. Cut into squares to serve.

COOK'S TIP

If liked, you can line the tin (pan) with baking parchment so that the biscuit can be lifted out before cutting into pieces.

Chocolate Chip Muffins

Muffins are always popular and are so simple to make. Mini muffins are fabulous bite-size treats or perfect for childrens parties.

NUTRITIONAL INFORMATION

Calories	318	Sugars	30g
Protein	5g	Fat	13g
Carbohydrate	48g	Saturates	5g

 20 MINS 30 MINS

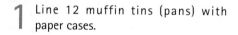

MAKES 12

I N G R E D I E N T S

100 g/3½ oz/generous ⅓ cup soft margarine

225 g/8 oz/1 cup caster (superfine) sugar

2 large eggs

150 ml/¼ pint/⅔ cup whole milk natural yogurt

5 tbsp milk

275 g/9½ oz/2 cups plain (all-purpose) flour

1 tsp bicarbonate of soda (baking soda)

175 g/6 oz dark chocolate chips

1 Line 12 muffin tins (pans) with paper cases.

2 Place the margarine and sugar in a large mixing bowl and beat with a wooden spoon until light and fluffy. Beat in the eggs, yogurt and milk until combined.

COOK'S TIP

For chocolate and orange muffins, add the grated rind of 1 orange and replace the milk with fresh orange juice.

3 Sieve (strain) the flour and bicarbonate of soda (baking soda) together and add to the mixture. Stir until just blended.

4 Stir in the chocolate chips, then spoon the mixture into the paper cases and bake in a preheated oven, 190°C/375°F/Gas Mark 5, for 25 minutes or until a fine skewer inserted into the centre comes out clean. Leave to cool in the tin (pan) for 5 minutes, then turn out on to a wire rack to cool completely.

Chocolate Crispy Bites

A favourite with children, this version of crispy bites have been given a new twist which is sure to be popular.

NUTRITIONAL INFORMATION

Calories	175	Sugars	14g
Protein	2g	Fat	10g
Carbohydrate	20g	Saturates	6g

 15 MINS   10 MINS

MAKES 16

INGREDIENTS

WHITE LAYER

50 g/1¾ oz/4 tbsp butter

1 tbsp golden (light corn) syrup

150 g/5½ oz white chocolate

50 g/1¾ oz toasted rice cereal

DARK LAYER

50 g/1¾ oz/4 tbsp butter

2 tbsp golden (light corn) syrup

125 g/dark chocolate, broken into small pieces

75 g/2¾ oz toasted rice cereal

1 Grease a 20 cm/8 inch square cake tin (pan) and line with baking parchment.

2 To make the white chocolate layer, melt the butter, golden (light corn) syrup and chocolate in a bowl set over a saucepan of gently simmering water.

3 Remove from the heat and stir in the rice cereal until it is well combined .

4 Press into the prepared tin (pan) and level the surface.

5 To make the dark chocolate layer, melt the butter, golden (light corn) syrup and dark chocolate in a bowl set over a pan of gently simmering water.

6 Remove from the heat and stir in the rice cereal until it is well coated. Pour the dark chocolate layer over the hardened white chocolate layer and chill until the top layer has hardened.

7 Turn out of the cake tin (pan) and cut into small squares, using a sharp knife.

COOK'S TIP

These bites can be made up to 4 days ahead. Keep them covered in the refrigerator until ready to use.

No-Bake Chocolate Squares

These are handy little squares to keep in the refrigerator for when unexpected guests arrive. Children also enjoy making them.

NUTRITIONAL INFORMATION

Calories 273	Sugars 23g
Protein 2g	Fat 16g
Carbohydrate ... 31g	Saturates 10g

  2 HR 20 MINS   0 MINS

MAKES 16

INGREDIENTS

275 g/9½ oz dark chocolate

175 g/6 oz/¾ cup butter

4 tbsp golden (light corn) syrup

2 tbsp dark rum (optional)

175 g/6 oz plain biscuits (cookies), such as Rich Tea

25 g/1 oz toasted rice cereal

50 g/1¾ oz/½ cup chopped walnuts or pecan nuts

100 g/3½ oz/½ cup glacé (candied) cherries, chopped roughly

25 g/1 oz white chocolate, to decorate

1 Place the dark chocolate in a large mixing bowl with the butter, syrup and rum, if using, and set over a saucepan of gently simmering water until melted, stirring until blended.

2 Break the biscuits (cookies) into small pieces and stir into the chocolate mixture along with the rice cereal, nuts and cherries.

3 Line a 18 cm/7inch square cake tin (pan) with baking parchment. Pour the mixture into the tin (pan) and level the top, pressing down well with the back of a spoon. Chill for 2 hours.

4 To decorate, melt the white chocolate and drizzle it over the top of the cake in a random pattern. Leave to set. To serve, carefully turn out of the tin (pan) and remove the baking parchment. Cut into 16 squares.

VARIATION

Brandy or an orange-flavoured liqueur can be used instead of the rum, if you prefer. Cherry brandy also works well. For a coconut flavour, replace the rice cereal with desiccated (shredded) coconut and add a coconut-flavoured liqueur.

Chocolate Scones

A plain scone mixture is transformed into a chocoholics treat by the simple addition of chocolate chips.

NUTRITIONAL INFORMATION

Calories	 176	Sugars 7g
Protein	.... 3g	Fat 8g
Carbohydrate	... 26g	Saturates 5g

 15 MINS   12 MINS

MAKES 9

I N G R E D I E N T S

225 g/8 oz/2 cups self-raising flour, sieved (strained)

60 g/2 oz/¼ cup butter

1 tbsp caster (superfine) sugar

50 g/1¾ oz/⅓ cup chocolate chips

about 150 ml/¼ pint/⅔ cup milk

1 Lightly grease a baking tray (cookie sheet). Place the flour in a mixing bowl. Cut the butter into small pieces and rub it into the flour with your fingertips until the scone mixture resembles fine breadcrumbs.

2 Stir in the caster (superfine) sugar and chocolate chips.

3 Mix in enough milk to form a soft dough.

4 On a lightly floured surface, roll out the dough to form a rectangle 10 × 15 cm/4 × 6 inches, about 2.5 cm/1 inch thick. Cut the dough into 9 squares.

5 Place the scones spaced well apart on the prepared baking tray (cookie sheet).

6 Brush with a little milk and bake in a preheated oven, 220°C/425°F/Gas Mark 7, for 10–12 minutes until the scones are risen and golden.

COOK'S TIP

To be at their best, all scones should be freshly baked and served warm. Split the warm scones and spread them with a little chocolate and hazelnut spread or a good dollop of whipped cream.

Pecan & Fudge Ring

Although this can be served cold as a cake, it is absolutely delicious served hot as a pudding.

NUTRITIONAL INFORMATION

Calories	518	Sugars	43g
Protein	7g	Fat	30g
Carbohydrate	59g	Saturates	9g

25 MINS   40 MINS

SERVES 6

INGREDIENTS

FUDGE SAUCE

40 g/1½ oz/3 tbsp butter

40 g/1½ oz/3 tbsp light muscovado sugar

4 tbsp golden (light corn) syrup

2 tbsp milk

1 tbsp cocoa powder

40 g/1½ oz dark chocolate

50 g/1¾ oz pecan nuts, finely chopped

CAKE

100 g/3½ oz/generous ⅓ cup soft margarine

100 g/3½ oz/7 tbsp light muscovado sugar

125 g/4½ oz/1 cup self-raising flour

2 eggs

2 tbsp milk

1 tbsp golden (light corn) syrup

COOK'S TIP

To make in the microwave, place the butter, sugar, syrup, milk and cocoa powder in a microwave-proof bowl. Cook on HIGH for 2 minutes, stir twice. Stir in the chocolate until melted, add the nuts. Pour into a 1.1 litre/2 pint/5 cup microwave-proof ring mould (mold). Make the cake and cook on HIGH for 3–4 minutes until just dry on top; stand for 5 minutes.

1 Lightly grease a 20 cm/8 inch ring tin (pan).

2 To make the fudge sauce, place the butter, sugar, syrup, milk and cocoa powder in a small pan and heat gently, stirring until combined.

3 Break the chocolate into pieces, add to the mixture and stir until melted. Stir in the chopped nuts. Pour into the base of the tin (pan) and leave to cool.

4 To make the cake, place all of the ingredients in a mixing bowl and beat until smooth. Carefully spoon the cake mixture over the chocolate fudge sauce.

5 Bake in a preheated oven, 180°C/350°F/Gas Mark 4, for 35 minutes or until the cake is springy to the touch.

6 Leave to cool in the tin (pan) for 5 minutes, then turn out on to a serving dish and serve.

Chocolate Apple Pie

Easy-to-make crumbly chocolate pastry encases a delicious apple filling studded with chocolate chips. Guaranteed to become a family favourite.

NUTRITIONAL INFORMATION

Calories 448	Sugars 26g
Protein 8g	Fat 24g
Carbohydrate ...53g	Saturates 15g

55 MINS   40 MINS

SERVES 6

I N G R E D I E N T S

CHOCOLATE PASTRY

4 tbsp cocoa powder

200 g/7 oz/1¾ cups plain (all-purpose) flour

2 egg yolks

100 g/3½ oz/¾ cup softened butter

50 g/1¾ oz/4 tbsp caster (superfine) sugar

few drops of vanilla flavouring (extract)

cold water, to mix

FILLING

750 g/1 lb 10 oz cooking apples

25 g/1 oz/2 tbsp butter

½ tsp ground cinnamon

50 g/1¾ oz/¾ cup dark chocolate chips

a little egg white, beaten

½ tsp caster (superfine) sugar

whipped cream or vanilla ice cream, to serve

1 To make the pastry, sieve (strain) the cocoa powder and flour into a mixing bowl and rub in the butter until the mixture resembles fine breadcrumbs. Stir in the sugar. Add the egg yolk, vanilla flavouring (extract) and enough water to mix to a dough.

2 Roll out the dough on a lightly floured surface and use to line a deep 20 cm/8 inch flan or cake tin (pan). Chill for 30 minutes. Roll out any trimmings and cut out some pastry leaves to decorate the top of the pie.

3 Peel, core and thickly slice the apples. Place half of the apple slices in a saucepan with the butter and cinnamon and cook over a gently heat, stirring occasionally until the apples soften.

4 Stir in the uncooked apple slices, leave to cool slightly, then stir in the chocolate chips. Prick the base of the pastry case (pie shell) and pile the apple mixture into it. Arrange the pastry leaves on top. Brush the leaves with a little egg white and sprinkle with caster (superfine) sugar.

5 Bake in a preheated oven, 180°C/350°F/Gas Mark 4, for 35 minutes until the pastry is crisp. Serve warm or cold, with whipped cream or vanilla ice cream.

Chocolate Fudge Pudding

This fabulous pudding is perfect for cold winter days – and it can be made in double quick time in the microwave, if you have one.

NUTRITIONAL INFORMATION

Calories 645   Sugars 43g
Protein . . . . 10g   Fat 42g
Carbohydrate . . . 62g   Saturates 16g

 25 MINS   1¾ HOURS

SERVES 6

I N G R E D I E N T S

150 g/5½ oz/generous ⅓ cup soft margarine

150 g/5½ oz/1¼ cups self-raising flour

150 g/5½ oz/½ cup golden (light corn) syrup

3 eggs

25 g/1 oz/¼ cup cocoa powder

CHOCOLATE FUDGE SAUCE

100 g/3½ oz dark chocolate

125 ml/4 fl oz/½ cup sweetened condensed milk

4 tbsp double (heavy) cream

1 Lightly grease a 1.2 litre/2 pint/5 cup pudding basin.

2 Place the ingredients for the sponge in a mixing bowl and beat until well combined and smooth.

3 Spoon into the prepared basin and level the top. Cover with a disc of baking parchment and tie a pleated sheet of foil over the basin. Steam for 1½–2 hours until the pudding is cooked and springy to the touch.

4 To make the sauce, break the chocolate into small pieces and place in a small pan with the condensed milk. Heat gently, stirring until the chocolate melts.

5 Remove the pan from the heat and stir in the double (heavy) cream.

6 To serve the pudding, turn it out on to a serving plate and pour over a little of the chocolate fudge sauce. Serve the remaining sauce separately.

COOK'S TIP

To cook in the microwave, cook it, uncovered, on HIGH for 4 minutes, turning once. Leave to stand for at least 5 minutes before turning out. Whilst it is standing, make the sauce. Break the chocolate into pieces and place in a microwave-proof bowl with the milk. Cook on HIGH for 1 minute, then stir until the chocolate melts. Stir in the double (heavy) cream and serve.

Chocolate Queen of Puddings

An old time favourite with an up-to-date twist, this pudding makes the perfect end to special family meal.

NUTRITIONAL INFORMATION

Calories .... 477 Sugars 68g
Protein .... 11g Fat 11g
Carbohydrate ... 88g Saturates 6g

25 MINS   40 MINS

SERVES 4

INGREDIENTS

50 g/1¾ oz dark chocolate

450 ml/16 fl oz/2 cups chocolate-flavoured milk

100 g/3½ oz/1¾ cups fresh white or wholemeal (whole wheat) breadcrumbs

125 g/4½ oz/½ cup caster (superfine) sugar

2 eggs, separated

4 tbsp black cherry jam

1 Break the chocolate into small pieces and place in a saucepan with the chocolate-flavoured milk. Heat gently, stirring until the chocolate melts. Bring almost to the boil, then remove the pan from the heat.

2 Place the breadcrumbs in a large mixing bowl with 25 g/1 oz/5 tsp of the sugar. Pour over the chocolate milk and mix well. Beat in the egg yolks.

3 Spoon into a 1.1 litre/2 pint/5 cup pie dish and bake in a preheated oven, 180°C/350°F/ Gas Mark 4, for 25–30 minutes or until set and firm to the touch.

4 Whisk the egg whites in a large grease-free bowl until standing in

soft peaks. Gradually whisk in the remaining caster (superfine) sugar and whisk until you have a glossy, thick meringue.

5 Spread the black cherry jam over the surface of the chocolate mixture and pile or pipe the meringue on top. Return the pudding to the oven for about 15 minutes or until the meringue is crisp and golden.

VARIATION

If you prefer, add 40 g/1½ oz/½ cup desiccated (shredded) coconut to the breadcrumbs and omit the jam.

Chocolate Fondue

This is a fun dessert to serve at the end of the meal. Prepare in advance, then just warm through before serving.

NUTRITIONAL INFORMATION

Calories	372	Sugars	29g
Protein	3g	Fat	27g
Carbohydrate	30g	Saturates	16g

10 MINS   10 MINS

SERVES 6

I N G R E D I E N T S

CHOCOLATE FONDUE

225 g/8 oz dark chocolate

200 ml/7 fl oz/¾ cup double (heavy) cream

2 tbsp brandy

TO SERVE

selection of fruit

white and pink marshmallows

sweet biscuits (cookies)

1 Break the chocolate into small pieces and place in a small saucepan with the double (heavy) cream.

2 Heat the mixture gently, stirring constantly until the chocolate has melted and blended with the cream.

3 Remove the pan from the heat and stir in the brandy.

4 Pour into a fondue pot or a small flameproof dish and keep warm, preferably over a small burner.

5 Serve with a selection of fruit, marshmallows and biscuits (cookies) for dipping. The fruit and marshmallows can be spiked on fondue forks, wooden skewers or ordinary forks for dipping into the chocolate fondue.

COOK'S TIP

Dish warmers which use a night light are just as good as a fondue set for keeping the fondue warm. If you do not have one, stand the fondue dish in a larger dish and pour in enough boiling water to come halfway up the fondue dish. Whichever method you use place your fondue on a heatproof stand to protect the table.

Hot Chocolate Soufflé

Served with hot chocolate custard this is a chocoholic's dream. Do not be put off by the mystique of soufflés – this one really is easy to make.

NUTRITIONAL INFORMATION

Calories 629   Sugars 49g
Protein . . . . 18g   Fat 33g
Carbohydrate . . . 70g   Saturates 18g

🕒 25 MINS   🕐 45 MINS

SERVES 4

I N G R E D I E N T S

100 g/3½ oz dark chocolate

300 ml/½ pint/1¼ cups milk

25 g/1 oz/2 tbsp butter

4 large eggs, separated

1 tbsp cornflour (cornstarch)

50 g/1¾ oz/4 tbsp caster (superfine) sugar

½ tsp vanilla flavouring (extract)

100 g/3½ oz/⅔ cup dark chocolate chips

caster (superfine) and icing (confectioners') sugar, to dust

C H O C O L A T E   C U S T A R D

2 tbsp cornflour (cornstarch)

1 tbsp caster (superfine) sugar

450 ml/¾ pint/2 cups milk

50 g/1¾ oz dark chocolate

1 Grease an 850 ml/1½ pint/ 5 cup soufflé dish and sprinkle with caster (superfine) sugar. Break the chocolate into pieces.

2 Heat the milk with the butter in a pan until almost boiling. Mix the egg yolks, cornflour (cornstarch) and caster (superfine) sugar in a bowl and pour on some of the hot milk, whisking. Return it to the pan and cook gently, stirring constantly until thickened. Add the chocolate and stir until melted. Remove from the heat and stir in the flavouring (extract).

3 Whisk the egg whites until standing in soft peaks. Fold half of the egg whites into the chocolate mixture. Fold in the rest with the chocolate chips. Pour into the dish and bake in a preheated oven, 180°C/350°F/Gas Mark 4, for 40–45 minutes until well risen.

4 Meanwhile, make the custard. Put the cornflour (cornstarch) and sugar in a small bowl and mix to a smooth paste with a little of the milk. Heat the remaining milk until almost boiling. Pour a little of the hot milk on to the cornflour (cornstarch), mix well, then pour back into the pan. Cook gently, stirring until thickened. Break the chocolate into pieces and add to the custard, stirring until melted.

5 Dust the soufflé with sugar and serve immediately with the chocolate custard.

Chocolate & Ginger Puddings

Individual puddings always look more professional and are quicker to cook. If you do not have mini pudding basins, use small teacups instead.

NUTRITIONAL INFORMATION

Calories	699	Sugars	61g
Protein	13g	Fat	38g
Carbohydrate	81g	Saturates	13g

25 MINS   50 MINS

SERVES 4

I N G R E D I E N T S

100 g/3½ oz/generous ⅓ cup soft margarine

100 g/3½ oz/¾ cup self-raising flour, sieved (strained)

100 g/3½ oz/7 tbsp caster (superfine) sugar

2 eggs

25 g/1 oz/¼ cup cocoa powder, sieved (strained)

25 g/1 oz dark chocolate

50 g/1¾ oz stem ginger

C H O C O L A T E   C U S T A R D

2 egg yolks

1 tbsp caster (superfine) sugar

1 tbsp cornflour (cornstarch)

300 ml/½ pint/1¼ cups milk

100 g/3½ oz dark chocolate, broken into pieces

icing (confectioners') sugar, to dust

1 Lightly grease 4 individual pudding basins. Place the margarine, flour, sugar, eggs and cocoa powder in a mixing bowl and beat until well combined and smooth. Chop the chocolate and ginger and stir into the mixture.

2 Spoon the cake mixture into the prepared basins and level the top. The mixture should three-quarters fill the basins. Cover the basins with discs of baking parchment and cover with a pleated sheet of foil. Steam for 45 minutes until the puddings are cooked and springy to the touch.

3 Meanwhile, make the custard. Beat together the egg yolks, sugar and cornflour (cornstarch) to form a smooth paste. Heat the milk until boiling and pour over the egg mixture. Return to the pan and cook over a very low heat stirring until thick. Remove from the heat and beat in the chocolate. Stir until the chocolate melts.

4 Lift the puddings from the steamer, run a knife around the edge of the basins and turn out on to serving plates. Dust with sugar and drizzle some chocolate custard over the top. Serve the remaining custard separately.

Bread & Butter Pudding

An old favourite is given a new twist! The brioche gives it a lovely rich flavour, but this recipe also works well with soft-baked batch bread.

NUTRITIONAL INFORMATION

Calories	525	Sugars	32g
Protein	20g	Fat	26g
Carbohydrate	56g	Saturates	12g

  20 MINS ⊘ 35 MINS

SERVES 4

I N G R E D I E N T S

225 g/8 oz brioche

15 g/½ oz/1 tbsp butter

50 g/1¾ oz dark chocolate chips

1 egg

2 egg yolks

50 g/1¾ oz/4 tbsp caster (superfine) sugar

410 g/15 oz can light evaporated milk

1 Cut the brioche into thin slices. Lightly butter one side of each slice.

2 Place a layer of brioche, buttered-side down, in the bottom of a shallow ovenproof dish. Sprinkle a few chocolate chips over the top.

3 Continue layering the brioche and chocolate chips, finishing with a layer of bread on top.

4 Whisk together the egg, egg yolks and sugar until well combined. Heat the milk in a small saucepan until it just begins to simmer. Gradually add to the egg mixture, whisking well.

5 Pour the custard over the pudding and leave to stand for 5 minutes. Press the brioche down into the milk.

6 Place in a roasting tin (pan) and fill with boiling water to come halfway up the side of the dish (this is known as a bain-marie).

7 Bake in a preheated oven, 180°C/350°F/Gas Mark 4, for 30 minutes or until the custard has set. Leave to cool for 5 minutes before serving.

VARIATION

For a double-chocolate pudding, heat the milk with 1 tbsp of cocoa powder, stirring until well dissolved then continue from step 4.

Chocolate & Banana Pancakes

Pancakes are given the chocolate treatment to make a rich and fabulous dessert. Prepare this recipe ahead of time for trouble-free entertaining.

NUTRITIONAL INFORMATION

Calories 379   Sugars 21g
Protein .... 10g   Fat 18g
Carbohydrate ... 46g   Saturates 7g

25 MINS   15 MINS

SERVES 4

I N G R E D I E N T S

3 large bananas

6 tbsp orange juice

grated rind of 1 orange

2 tbsp orange – or banana-flavoured liqueur

HOT CHOCOLATE SAUCE

1 tbsp cocoa powder

2 tsp cornflour (cornstarch)

3 tbsp milk

40 g/1½ oz dark chocolate

15 g/½ oz/1 tbsp butter

175 g/6 oz/½ cup golden (light corn) syrup

¼ tsp vanilla flavouring (extract)

PANCAKES

100 g/3½ oz/1 cup plain (all-purpose) flour

1 tbsp cocoa powder

1 egg

1 tsp sunflower oil

300 ml/½ pint/1¼ cups milk

oil, for frying

1 Peel and slice the bananas and arrange them in a dish with the orange juice and rind and the liqueur. Set aside.

2 Mix the cocoa powder and cornflour (cornstarch) in a bowl, then stir in the milk. Break the dark chocolate into pieces and place in a pan with the butter and golden (light corn) syrup. Heat gently, stirring until well blended. Add the cocoa mixture and bring to the boil over a gentle heat, stirring. Simmer for 1 minute, then remove from the heat and stir in the vanilla flavouring (extract).

3 To make the pancakes, sieve (strain) the flour and cocoa into a mixing bowl and make a well in the centre. Add the egg and oil. Gradually whisk in the milk to form a smooth batter. Heat a little oil in a heavy-based frying pan (skillet) and pour off any excess. Pour in a little batter and tilt the pan to coat the base. Cook over a medium heat until the underside is browned. Flip over and cook the other side. Slide the pancake out of the pan and keep warm. Repeat until all the batter has been used.

4 To serve, reheat the chocolate sauce for 1–2 minutes. Fill the pancakes with the bananas and fold in half or into triangles. Pour over a little chocolate sauce and serve.

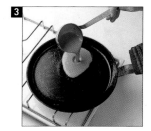

Chocolate Meringue Pie

Crumbly biscuit base, rich creamy chocolate filling topped with fluffy meringue – what could be more indulgent than this fabulous dessert?

NUTRITIONAL INFORMATION

Calories 581   Sugars 52g
Protein . . . . 9g   Fat 25g
Carbohydrate . . . 85g   Saturates 14g

30 MINS   35 MINS

SERVES 6

INGREDIENTS

225 g/8 oz dark chocolate digestive biscuits (graham crackers)

50 g/1¾ oz/4 tbsp butter

FILLING

3 egg yolks

50 g/1¾ oz/4 tbsp caster (superfine) sugar

4 tbsp cornflour (cornstarch)

600 ml/1 pint/2½ cups milk

100 g/3½ oz dark chocolate, melted

MERINGUE

2 egg whites

100 g/3½ oz/7 tbsp caster (superfine) sugar

¼ tsp vanilla flavouring (extract)

1 Place the digestive biscuits (graham crackers) in a plastic bag and crush with a rolling pin. Pour into a mixing bowl. Melt the butter and stir it into the biscuit (cracker) crumbs until well mixed. Press the biscuit mixture firmly into the base and up the sides of a 23 cm/9 inch flan tin (pan) or dish.

2 To make the filling, beat the egg yolks, caster (superfine) sugar and cornflour (cornstarch) in a large bowl until they form a smooth paste, adding a little of the milk if necessary. Heat the milk until almost boiling, then slowly pour it on to the egg mixture, whisking well.

3 Return the mixture to the saucepan and cook gently, whisking constantly until it thickens. Remove from the heat. Whisk in the melted chocolate, then pour it on to the digestive biscuit (graham cracker) base.

4 To make the meringue, whisk the egg whites in a large mixing bowl until standing in soft peaks. Gradually whisk in about two-thirds of the sugar until the mixture is stiff and glossy. Fold in the remaining sugar and vanilla flavouring (extract).

5 Spread the meringue over the filling, swirling the surface with the back of a spoon to give it an attractive finish. Bake in the centre of a preheated oven, 170°C/375°F/Gas Mark 3, for 30 minutes or until the meringue is golden. Serve hot or just warm.

Chocolate Cheesecake

This cheesecake takes a little time to prepare and cook but is well worth the effort. It is quite rich and is good served with a little fresh fruit.

NUTRITIONAL INFORMATION

Calories 471   Sugars 20g
Protein . . . . .10g   Fat 33g
Carbohydrate . . .28g   Saturates 5g

15 MINS   1¼ HOURS

SERVES 12

I N G R E D I E N T S

100 g/3½ oz/¾ cup plain (all-purpose) flour

100 g/3½ oz/¾ cup ground almonds

200 g/7 oz/¾ cup demerara (brown crystal) sugar

150 g/5½ oz/11 tbsp margarine

675 g/1½ lb firm tofu (bean curd)

175 ml/6 fl oz/¾ cup vegetable oil

125 ml/4 fl oz/½ cup orange juice

175 ml/6 fl oz/¾ cup brandy

50 g/1¾ oz/6 tbsp cocoa powder, (unsweetened cocoa), plus extra to decorate

2 tsp almond essence (extract)

icing (confectioners') sugar and Cape gooseberries (ground cherries), to decorate

1 Put the flour, ground almonds and 1 tablespoon of the sugar in a bowl and mix well. Rub the margarine into the mixture to form a dough.

2 Lightly grease and line the base of a 23 cm/9 inch springform tin (pan). Press the dough into the base of the tin (pan) to cover, pushing the dough right up to the edge of the tin (pan).

3 Roughly chop the tofu (bean curd) and put in a food processor with the vegetable oil, orange juice, brandy, cocoa powder (unsweetened cocoa) almond essence and remaining sugar and process until smooth and creamy. Pour over the base in the tin (pan) and cook in a preheated oven, 160°C/325°F/ Gas Mark 3, for 1–1¼ hours, or until set.

4 Leave to cool in the tin (pan) for 5 minutes, then remove from the tin (pan) and chill in the refrigerator. Dust with icing (confectioners') sugar and cocoa powder (unsweetened cocoa). Decorate with Cape gooseberries (ground cherries) and serve.

COOK'S TIP

Cape gooseberries (ground cherries) make an attractive decoration for many desserts. Peel open the papery husks to expose the bright orange fruits.

Marble Cheesecake

A dark and white chocolate cheesecake filling is marbled together to a give an attractive finish to this rich and decadent dessert.

NUTRITIONAL INFORMATION

Calories 690   Sugars 40g
Protein . . . . 9g   Fat 51g
Carbohydrate . . . 53g   Saturates 29g

🍲 25 MINS   🕐 0 MINS

SERVES 10

I N G R E D I E N T S

BASE

225 g/8 oz toasted oat cereal

50 g/1¾ oz/½ cup toasted hazelnuts, chopped

50 g/1¾ oz/4 tbsp butter

25 g/1 oz dark chocolate

FILLING

350 g/12 oz full fat soft cheese

100 g/3½ oz/7 tbsp caster (superfine) sugar

200 ml/7 fl oz/¾ cup thick yogurt

300 ml/½ pint/1¼ cups double (heavy) cream

1 sachet (envelope) gelatine

3 tbsp water

175 g/6 oz dark chocolate, melted

175 g/6 oz white chocolate, melted

COOK'S TIP

For a lighter texture, fold in 2 egg whites whipped to soft peaks before folding in the cream in step 4.

1 Place the toasted oat cereal in a plastic bag and crush with a rolling pin. Pour the crushed cereal into a mixing bowl and stir in the hazelnuts.

2 Melt the butter and chocolate together over a low heat and stir into the cereal mixture, stirring until well coated.

3 Using the bottom of a glass, press the mixture into the base and up the sides of a 20 cm/8 inch springform tin (pan).

4 Beat together the cheese and sugar with a wooden spoon until smooth.

Beat in the yogurt. Whip the cream until just holding its shape and fold into the mixture. Sprinkle the gelatine over the water in a heatproof bowl and leave to go spongy. Place over a pan of hot water and stir until dissolved. Stir into the mixture.

5 Divide the mixture in half and beat the dark chocolate into one half and the white chocolate into the other half.

6 Place alternate spoonfuls of mixture on top of the cereal base. Swirl the filling together with the tip of a knife to give a marbled effect. Level the top with a scraper or a palette knife (spatula). Leave to chill until set before serving.

Chocolate Mint Swirl

The classic combination of chocolate and mint flavours makes an attractive dessert for special occasions.

NUTRITIONAL INFORMATION

Calories	424	Sugars	26g
Protein	4g	Fat	34g
Carbohydrate	26g	Saturates	21g

 20 MINS   0 MINS

SERVES 6

INGREDIENTS

300 ml/½ pint/1¼ cups double (heavy) cream

150 ml/¼ pint/⅔ cup creamy fromage frais

25 g/1 oz/2 tbsp icing (confectioners') sugar

1 tbsp crème de menthe

175 g/6 oz dark chocolate

chocolate, to decorate

1 Place the cream in a large mixing bowl and whisk until standing in soft peaks.

2 Fold in the fromage frais and icing (confectioners') sugar, then place about one-third of the mixture in a smaller bowl. Stir the crème de menthe into the smaller bowl. Melt the dark chocolate and stir it into the remaining mixture.

3 Place alternate spoonfuls of the 2 mixtures into serving glasses, then swirl the mixture together to give a decorative effect. Leave to chill until required.

4 To make the piped chocolate decorations, melt a small amount of chocolate and place in a paper piping bag.

5 Place a sheet of baking parchment on a board and pipe squiggles, stars or flower shapes with the melted chocolate. Alternatively, to make curved decorations, pipe decorations on to a long strip of baking parchment, then carefully place the strip over a rolling pin, securing with sticky tape. Leave the chocolate to set, then carefully remove from the baking parchment.

6 Decorate each dessert with piped chocolate decorations and serve. The desserts can be decorated and then chilled, if preferred.

COOK'S TIP

Pipe the patterns freehand or draw patterns on to baking parchment first, turn the parchment over and then pipe the chocolate, following the drawn outline.

Mississippi Mud Pie

An all-time favourite with chocoholics – the 'mud' refers to the gooey, rich chocolate layer of the cake.

NUTRITIONAL INFORMATION

Calories 1120	Sugars 68g	
Protein 13g	Fat 81g	
Carbohydrate ... 91g	Saturates 51g	

 25 MINS   1¼ HOURS

SERVES 8

I N G R E D I E N T S

225 g/8 oz/2 cups plain (all-purpose) flour

25 g/1 oz/¼ cup cocoa powder

150 g/5½ oz/⅔ cup butter

25 g/1 oz/5 tsp caster (superfine) sugar

about 2 tbsp cold water

F I L L I N G

175 g/6 oz/¾ cup butter

350 g/12 oz dark muscovado sugar

4 eggs, lightly beaten

4 tbsp cocoa powder, sieved (strained)

150 g/5½ oz dark chocolate

300ml/½ pt single (light) cream

1 tsp chocolate flavouring (extract)

T O   D E C O R A T E

425 ml/¾ pint/1¾ cups double (heavy) cream, whipped

thick bar of chocolate

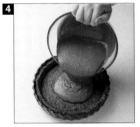  

1 To make the pastry (pie dough), sieve (strain) the flour and cocoa powder into a mixing bowl. Rub in the butter until the mixture resembles fine breadcrumbs. Stir in the sugar and enough cold water to mix to a soft dough. Chill for 15 minutes.

2 Roll out the dough on a lightly floured surface and use to line a deep 23 cm/9 inch loose-bottomed flan tin (pan) or ceramic flan dish. Line with foil or baking parchment and baking beans. Bake blind in a preheated oven, 190°C/375°F/Gas Mark 5, for 15 minutes. Remove the beans and foil or paper and cook for a further 10 minutes until crisp.

3 To make the filling, beat the butter and sugar in a bowl and gradually beat in the eggs with the cocoa powder. Melt the chocolate and beat it into the mixture with the single (light) cream and the chocolate flavouring (extract).

4 Pour the mixture into the cooked pastry case and bake at 170°C/325°F/Gas Mark 3 for 45 minutes or until the filling is set.

5 Leave to cool completely, then transfer the pie to a serving plate, if preferred. Cover with the whipped cream and leave to chill.

6 To make small chocolate curls, use a potato peeler to remove curls from the bar of chocolate. Decorate the pie and leave to chill.

Champagne Mousse

A wonderful champagne-flavoured mousse is served in chocolate sponge cups for an elegant dessert. Any dry sparkling wine can be used.

NUTRITIONAL INFORMATION

Calories	850	Sugars	57g
Protein	15g	Fat	52g
Carbohydrate	72g	Saturates	30g

35 MINS   10 MINS

SERVES 4

I N G R E D I E N T S

SPONGE

4 eggs

100 g/3½ oz/7 tbsp caster (superfine) sugar

75 g/2¾ oz/⅔ cup self-raising flour

15 g/¼ oz/2 tbsp cocoa powder

25 g/1 oz/2 tbsp butter, melted

MOUSSE

1 sachet (envelope) gelatine

3 tbsp water

300 ml/½ pint/1¼ cups champagne

300 ml/½ pint/1¼ cups double (heavy) cream

2 egg whites

75 g/2¾ oz/⅓ cup caster (superfine) sugar

TO DECORATE

50 g/2 oz dark chocolate-flavoured cake covering, melted

fresh strawberries

1 Line a 37.5 × 25 cm/15 × 10 inch Swiss roll tin (pan) with greased baking parchment. Place the eggs and sugar in a bowl and whisk with electric beaters until the mixture is very thick and the whisk leaves a trail when lifted. If using a balloon whisk, stand the bowl over a pan of hot water whilst whisking. Sieve (strain) the flour and cocoa together and fold into the egg mixture. Fold in the butter. Pour into the tin (pan) and bake in a preheated oven, 200°C/400°F/Gas Mark 6, for 8 minutes or until springy to the touch. Cool for 5 minutes, then turn out on to a wire rack until cold. Line four 10 cm/4 inch baking rings with baking parchment. Line the sides with 2.5 cm/1 inch strips of cake and the base with circles.

2 To make the mousse, sprinkle the gelatine over the water and leave to go spongy. Place the bowl over a pan of hot water; stir until dissolved. Stir in the champagne.

3 Whip the cream until just holding its shape. Fold in the champagne mixture. Leave in a cool place until on the point of setting, stirring. Whisk the egg whites until standing in soft peaks, add the sugar and whisk until glossy. Fold into the setting mixture. Spoon into the sponge cases, allowing the mixture to go above the sponge. Chill for 2 hours. Pipe the cake covering in squiggles on a piece of parchment; leave to set. Decorate the mousses.

Chocolate Rum Pots

Wickedly rich little pots, flavoured with a hint of dark rum, for pure indulgence!

NUTRITIONAL INFORMATION

Calories 351	Sugars 37g	
Protein 2g	Fat 20g	
Carbohydrate . . . 37g	Saturates 12g	

 20 MINS   0 MINS

SERVES 6

I N G R E D I E N T S

225 g/8 oz dark chocolate

4 eggs, separated

75 g/2¾ oz/⅓ cup caster (superfine) sugar

4 tbsp dark rum

4 tbsp double (heavy) cream

TO DECORATE

a little whipped cream

chocolate shapes (see page 61)

1 Melt the chocolate and leave to cool slightly.

2 Whisk the egg yolks with the caster (superfine) sugar in a bowl until very pale and fluffy; this will take about 5 minutes with electric beaters, a little longer with a balloon whisk.

3 Drizzle the chocolate into the mixture and fold in together with the rum and the double (heavy) cream.

4 Whisk the egg whites in a grease-free bowl until standing in soft peaks. Fold the egg whites into the chocolate mixture in 2 batches. Divide the mixture between 6 ramekins (custard pots), or other individual dishes, and leave to chill for at least 2 hours.

5 To serve, decorate with a little whipped cream and small chocolate shapes.

COOK'S TIP

Make sure you use a perfectly clean and grease-free bowl for whisking the egg whites. They will not aerate if any grease is present as the smallest amount breaks down the bubbles in the whites, preventing them from trapping and holding air.

Chocolate Fruit Tartlets

Chocolate pastry trimmed with nuts makes a perfect case (shell) for fruit in these tasty individual tartlets. Use a variety of fruit.

NUTRITIONAL INFORMATION

Calories 510   Sugars 23g
Protein .... 8g   Fat 30g
Carbohydrate ... 56g   Saturates 17g

20 MINS   20 MINS

SERVES 6

INGREDIENTS

250 g/9 oz/1¼ cups plain (all-purpose) flour

3 tbsp cocoa powder

150 g/5½ oz/⅔ cup butter

40 g/1½ oz/3 tbsp caster (superfine) sugar

2–3 tbsp water

50 g/1¾ oz dark chocolate

50 g/1¾ oz/½ cup chopped mixed nuts, toasted

350 g/12 oz prepared fruit

3 tbsp apricot jam or redcurrant jelly

1 Sieve (strain) the flour and cocoa powder into a mixing bowl. Cut the butter into small pieces and rub into the flour with your fingertips until the mixture resembles fine breadcrumbs.

2 Stir in the sugar. Add enough of the water to mix to a soft dough, about 1–2 tablespoons. Cover and chill for 15 minutes.

3 Roll out the pastry (pie dough) on a lightly floured surface and use to line six 10 cm/4 inch tartlet tins (pans). Prick the pastry (pie dough) with a fork and line the pastry cases (pie shells) with a little crumpled foil. Bake in a preheated oven, 190°C/375°F/Gas Mark 5, for 10 minutes.

4 Remove the foil and bake for a further 5–10 minutes until the pastry

(pie dough) is crisp. Place the tins (pans) on a wire rack to cool completely.

5 Melt the chocolate. Spread out the chopped nuts on a plate. Remove the pastry cases (pie shells) from the tins (pans). Spread melted chocolate on the rims, then dip in the nuts. Leave to set.

6 Arrange the fruit in the tartlet cases (shells). Melt the apricot jam or redcurrant jelly with the remaining 1 tablespoon of water and brush it over the fruit. Chill the tartlets until required.

COOK'S TIP

If liked, you can fill the cases with a little sweetened cream before topping with the fruit. For a chocolate-flavoured filling, blend 225 g/8 oz chocolate hazelnut spread with 5 tablespoons of thick yogurt or whipped cream.

Chocolate & Vanilla Creams

These rich, creamy desserts are completely irresistible. Serve them with crisp dessert biscuits (cookies).

NUTRITIONAL INFORMATION

Calories	750	Sugars	32g
Protein	5g	Fat	67g
Carbohydrate	33g	Saturates	42g

45 MINS   0 MINS

SERVES 4

INGREDIENTS

450 ml/16 fl oz/2 cups double (heavy) cream

75 g/2¾ oz/⅓ cup caster (superfine) sugar

1 vanilla pod

200 ml/7 fl oz/¾ cup crème fraîche

2 tsp gelatine

3 tbsp water

50 g/1¾ oz dark chocolate

MARBLED CHOCOLATE SHAPES

a little melted white chocolate

a little melted dark chocolate

1   Place the cream and sugar in a saucepan. Cut the vanilla pod into 2 pieces and add to the cream. Heat gently, stirring until the sugar has dissolved, then bring to the boil. Reduce the heat and leave to simmer for 2–3 minutes.

2   Remove the pan from the heat and take out the vanilla pod. Stir in the crème fraîche.

3   Sprinkle the gelatine over the water in a small heatproof bowl and leave to go spongy, then place over a pan of hot water and stir until dissolved. Stir into the cream mixture. Pour half of this mixture into another mixing bowl.

4   Melt the dark chocolate and stir it into one half of the cream mixture. Pour the chocolate mixture into 4 individual glass serving dishes and chill for 15–20 minutes until just set. While it is chilling, keep the vanilla mixture at room temperature.

5   Spoon the vanilla mixture on top of the chocolate mixture and chill until the vanilla is set.

6   Meanwhile, make the shapes for the decoration. Spoon the melted white chocolate into a paper piping bag and snip off the tip. Spread some melted dark chocolate on a piece of baking parchment. Whilst still wet, pipe a fine line of white chocolate in a scribble over the top. Use the tip of a cocktail stick (toothpick) to marble the white chocolate into the dark. When firm but not too hard, cut into shapes with a small shaped cutter or a sharp knife. Chill the shapes until firm, then use to decorate the desserts.

Profiteroles & Banana Cream

Chocolate profiteroles are a popular choice. In this recipe they are filled with a delicious banana-flavoured cream.

NUTRITIONAL INFORMATION

Calories	858	Sugars	45g
Protein	9g	Fat	64g
Carbohydrate	63g	Saturates	39g

🍳 35 MINS   🕐 20 MINS

SERVES 4

I N G R E D I E N T S

CHOUX PASTRY (PIE DOUGH)

150 ml/¼ pint/⅔ cup water

60 g/2 oz/¼ cup butter

90 g/3 oz/¾ cup strong plain (all-purpose) flour, sieved (strained)

2 eggs

CHOCOLATE SAUCE

100 g/3½ oz dark chocolate, broken into pieces

2 tbsp water

50 g/1¾ oz/4 tbsp icing (confectioners') sugar

25 g/1 oz/2 tbsp unsalted butter

FILLING

300 ml/½ pint/1¼ cups double (heavy) cream

1 banana

25 g/1 oz/2 tbsp icing (confectioners') sugar

2 tbsp banana-flavoured liqueur

and add to the pan. Heat gently until the butter melts, then bring to a rolling boil. Remove the pan from the heat and add the flour in one go, beating well until the mixture leaves the sides of the pan and forms a ball. Leave to cool slightly, then gradually beat in the eggs to form a smooth, glossy mixture. Spoon the paste into a large piping bag fitted with a 1 cm/½ inch plain nozzle (tip).

2 Pipe about 18 small balls of the paste on to the baking tray (cookie sheet), allowing enough room for them to expand during cooking. Bake in a preheated oven, 220°C/425°F/Gas Mark 7, for 15–20 minutes until crisp and golden. Remove from the oven and make a small slit in each one for steam to escape. Cool on a wire rack.

3 To make the sauce, place all the ingredients in a heatproof bowl, set over a pan of simmering water and heat until combined to make a smooth sauce, stirring.

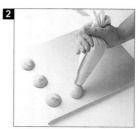

4 To make the filling, whip the cream until standing in soft peaks. Mash the banana with the sugar and liqueur. Fold into the cream. Place in a piping bag fitted with a 1 cm/½ inch plain nozzle (tip) and pipe into the profiteroles. Serve with the sauce poured over.

1 Lightly grease a baking tray (cookie sheet) and sprinkle with a little water. To make the pastry, place the water in a pan. Cut the butter into small pieces

Chocolate Marquise

This is a classic French dish, part way between a mousse and parfait.
It is usually chilled in a large mould (mold).

NUTRITIONAL INFORMATION

Calories 554	Sugars 23g
Protein 4g	Fat 50g
Carbohydrate ... 23g	Saturates 31g

25 MINS   0 MINS

SERVES 6

I N G R E D I E N T S

200 g/7 oz dark chocolate

100 g/3½ oz/generous ⅓ cup butter

3 egg yolks

75 g/2¾ oz/⅓ cup caster (superfine) sugar

1 tsp chocolate flavouring (extract) or 1 tbsp chocolate-flavoured liqueur

300 ml/½ pint/1¼ cups double (heavy) cream

TO SERVE

crème fraîche

chocolate-dipped fruits (see page 20)

cocoa powder, to dust

1 Break the chocolate into pieces. Place the chocolate and butter in a bowl over a pan of gently simmering water and stir until melted and well combined. Remove from the heat and leave to cool.

2 Place the egg yolks in a mixing bowl with the sugar and whisk until pale and fluffy. Using an electric whisk running on low speed, slowly whisk in the cool chocolate mixture. Stir in the chocolate flavouring (extract) or chocolate-flavoured liqueur.

3 Whip the cream until just holding its shape. Fold into the chocolate mixture. Spoon into 6 small ramekins

(custard pots), or individual metal moulds (molds). Leave to chill for at least 2 hours.

4 To serve, turn out the desserts on to individual serving dishes. If you have difficulty turning them out, dip the moulds (molds) into a bowl of warm water for a few seconds to help the marquise to slip out. Serve with chocolate-dipped fruit and crème fraîche and dust with cocoa powder.

COOK'S TIP

The slight tartness of the crème fraîche contrasts well with this very rich dessert. Dip the fruit in white chocolate to give a good colour contrast.

Tiramisu Layers

This is a modern version of the well-known and very traditional chocolate dessert from Italy.

NUTRITIONAL INFORMATION

Calories 798   Sugars 60g
Protein ....12g   Fat 50g
Carbohydrate ...76g   Saturates 25g

1¼ HOURS   5 MINS

SERVES 6

I N G R E D I E N T S

300 g/10½ oz dark chocolate

400 g/14 oz mascarpone cheese

150 ml/¼ pint/⅔ cup double (heavy) cream, whipped until it just holds its shape

400 ml/14 fl oz black coffee with 50 g/ 1¾ oz caster (superfine) sugar, cooled

6 tbsp dark rum or brandy

36 sponge fingers (lady-fingers), about 400 g/14 oz

cocoa powder, to dust

1 Melt the chocolate in a bowl set over a saucepan of simmering water, stirring occasionally. Leave the chocolate to cool slightly, then stir it into the mascarpone and cream.

2 Mix the coffee and rum together in a bowl. Dip the sponge fingers (lady-fingers) into the mixture briefly so that they absorb the coffee and rum liquid but do not become soggy.

3 Place 3 sponge fingers (lady-fingers) on 3 serving plates.

4 Spoon a layer of the mascarpone and chocolate mixture over the sponge fingers (lady-fingers).

5 Place 3 more sponge fingers (lady-fingers) on top of the mascarpone layer. Spread another layer of mascarpone and chocolate mixture and place 3 more sponge fingers (lady-fingers) on top.

6 Leave the tiramisu to chill in the refrigerator for at least 1 hour. Dust all over with a little cocoa powder just before serving.

VARIATION

Try adding 50 g/1¾ oz toasted, chopped hazelnuts to the chocolate cream mixture in step 1, if you prefer.

Iced White Chocolate Terrine

This iced dessert is somewhere between a chocolate mousse and an ice cream. Serve it with a chocolate sauce or a fruit coulis and fresh fruit.

NUTRITIONAL INFORMATION

Calories 420	Sugars 28g	
Protein 7g	Fat 32g	
Carbohydrate ... 28g	Saturates 19g	

30 MINS   0 MINS

SERVES 8

INGREDIENTS

2 tbsp granulated sugar

5 tbsp water

300 g/10½ oz white chocolate

3 eggs, separated

300 ml/½ pint/1¼ cups double (heavy) cream

1 Line a 450 g/1 lb loaf tin (pan) with foil or cling film (plastic wrap), pressing out as many creases as you can.

2 Place the granulated sugar and water in a heavy-based pan and heat gently, stirring until the sugar has dissolved. Bring to the boil and boil for 1–2 minutes until syrupy, then remove the pan from the heat.

3 Break the white chocolate into small pieces and stir it into the syrup, continuing to stir until the chocolate has melted and combined with the syrup. Leave to cool slightly.

4 Beat the egg yolks into the chocolate mixture. Leave to cool completely.

5 Lightly whip the cream until just holding its shape and fold it into the chocolate mixture.

6 Whisk the egg whites in a grease-free bowl until they are standing in soft peaks. Fold into the chocolate mixture. Pour into the prepared loaf tin (pan) and freeze overnight.

7 To serve, remove from the freezer about 10–15 minutes before serving. Turn out of the tin (pan) and cut into slices to serve.

COOK'S TIP

To make a coulis, place 225 g/ 8 oz soft fruit of your choice in a food processor or blender. Add 1–2 tbsp icing (confectioners') sugar and blend to form a purée. If the fruit contains seeds, push the purée through a sieve to remove them. Leave to chill until required.

Chocolate Charlotte

This chocolate dessert, consisting of a rich mousse-like filling enclosed in boudoir biscuits (lady-fingers), is a variation of a popular classic.

NUTRITIONAL INFORMATION

Calories	538	Sugars	53g
Protein	7g	Fat	32g
Carbohydrate	56g	Saturates	18g

25 MINS   0 MINS

SERVES 8

INGREDIENTS

about 22 boudoir biscuits (lady-fingers)

4 tbsp orange-flavoured liqueur

250 g/9 oz dark chocolate

150 ml/¼ pint double (heavy) cream

4 eggs

150 g/5½ oz/⅔ cup caster (superfine) sugar

TO DECORATE

150 ml/¼ pint/⅔ cup whipping cream

2 tbsp caster (superfine) sugar

½ tsp vanilla flavouring (extract)

large dark chocolate curls, (see page 57)

chocolate leaves (see page 23) or chocolate shapes (see page 61)

Use to line the sides of the mould (mold) or tin (pan), trimming if necessary to make a tight fit.

3 Break the chocolate into small pieces, place in a bowl and melt over a pan of hot water. Remove from the heat and stir in the double (heavy) cream.

4 Separate the eggs and place the whites in a large grease-free bowl. Beat the egg yolks into the chocolate mixture.

5 Whisk the egg whites until standing in stiff peaks, then gradually add the caster (superfine) sugar, whisking until stiff and glossy. Carefully fold the egg whites into the chocolate mixture in 2 batches, taking care not to knock out all of the air. Pour into the centre of the mould (mold). Trim the biscuits (lady-fingers) so that they are level with the chocolate mixture. Leave to chill for at least 5 hours.

6 To decorate, whisk the cream, sugar and vanilla flavouring (extract) until standing in soft peaks. Turn out the Charlotte on to a serving dish. Pipe cream rosettes around the base and decorate with chocolate curls and leaves.

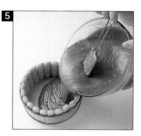

1 Line the base of a Charlotte mould (mold) or a deep 18 cm/7 inch round cake tin (pan) with a piece of baking parchment.

2 Place the boudoir biscuits (lady-fingers) on a tray and sprinkle with half of the orange-flavoured liqueur.

Chocolate Banana Sundae

A banana split in a glass! Choose the best vanilla ice cream you can find, or better still make your own.

NUTRITIONAL INFORMATION

Calories . . . . 778 Sugars 70g
Protein . . . . 11g Fat 47g
Carbohydrate . . . 81g Saturates 23g

20 MINS   0 MINS

SERVES 4

INGREDIENTS

GLOSSY CHOCOLATE SAUCE

60 g/2 oz dark chocolate

4 tbsp golden (light corn) syrup

15 g/½ oz/1 tbsp butter

1 tbsp brandy or rum (optional)

SUNDAE

4 bananas

150 ml/¼ pint/⅔ cup double (heavy) cream

8–12 scoops of good quality vanilla ice cream

75 g/2¾ oz/⅔ cup flaked (slivered) or chopped almonds, toasted

grated or flaked chocolate, to sprinkle

4 fan wafer biscuits (cookies)

1 To make the chocolate sauce, break the chocolate into small pieces and place in a heatproof bowl with the syrup and butter. Heat over a pan of hot water until melted, stirring until well combined. Remove the bowl from the heat and stir in the brandy or rum, if using.

2 Slice the bananas and whip the cream until just holding its shape.

Place a scoop of ice cream in the bottom of 4 tall sundae dishes. Top with slices of banana, some chocolate sauce, a spoonful of cream and a good sprinkling of nuts.

3 Repeat the layers, finishing with a good dollop of cream, sprinkled with nuts and a little grated or flaked chocolate. Serve with fan wafer biscuits (cookies).

VARIATION

For a traditional banana split, halve the bananas lengthways and place on a plate with two scoops of ice cream between. Top with cream and sprinkle with nuts. Serve with the glossy chocolate sauce poured over the top.

Black Forest Trifle

Try all the delightful flavours of a Black Forest Gateau in this new guise – the results are stunning.

NUTRITIONAL INFORMATION

Calories	585	Sugars	52g
Protein	8g	Fat	36g
Carbohydrate	61g	Saturates	19g

25 MINS   0 MINS

SERVES 6

I N G R E D I E N T S

6 thin slices chocolate butter cream Swiss roll

2 x 400 g/14 oz can black cherries

2 tbsp kirsch

1 tbsp cornflour (cornstarch)

2 tbsp caster (superfine) sugar

425 ml/¾ pint/1¾ cups milk

3 egg yolks

1 egg

75 g/2¾ oz dark chocolate

300 ml/½ pint/1¼ cups double (heavy) cream, lightly whipped

TO DECORATE

dark chocolate, melted

maraschino cherries (optional)

1 Place the slices of chocolate Swiss roll in the bottom of a glass serving bowl.

2 Drain the black cherries, reserving 6 tbsp of the juice. Place the cherries and the reserved juice on top of the cake. Sprinkle with the kirsch.

3 In a bowl, mix the cornflour (cornstarch) and caster (superfine) sugar. Stir in enough of the milk to mix to a smooth paste. Beat in the egg yolks and the whole egg.

4 Heat the remaining milk in a small saucepan until almost boiling, then gradually pour it on to the egg mixture, whisking well until it is combined.

5 Place the bowl over a pan of hot water and cook over a low heat until the custard thickens, stirring. Add the chocolate and stir until melted.

6 Pour the chocolate custard over the cherries and cool. When cold, spread the cream over the custard, swirling with the back of a spoon. Chill before decorating.

7 To make chocolate caraque, spread the melted dark chocolate on a marble or acrylic board. As it begins to set, pull a knife through the chocolate at a 45°C angle, working quickly. Remove each caraque as you make it and chill firmly before using.

Banana–Coconut Cheesecake

The combination of banana and coconut goes well with chocolate. You can use desiccated (shredded) coconut, but fresh will give a better flavour.

NUTRITIONAL INFORMATION

Calories 410	Sugars 27g
Protein 7g	Fat 27g
Carbohydrate . . . 40g	Saturates 15g

🍶 30 MINS   🕐 0 MINS

SERVES 10

I N G R E D I E N T S

225 g/8 oz chocolate chip cookies

50 g/1¾ oz/4 tbsp butter

350 g/12 oz medium-fat soft cheese

75 g/2¾ oz/⅓ cup caster (superfine) sugar

50 g/1¾ oz fresh coconut, grated

2 tbsp coconut-flavoured liqueur

2 ripe bananas

125 g/4½ oz dark chocolate

1 sachet (envelope) gelatine

3 tbsp water

150 ml/¼ pint/⅔ cup double (heavy) cream

T O   D E C O R A T E

1 banana

lemon juice

a little melted chocolate

COOK'S TIP

To crack the coconut, pierce 2 of the 'eyes' and drain off the liquid. Tap hard around the centre with a hammer until it cracks; lever apart.

 1 Place the biscuits (cookies) in a plastic bag and crush with a rolling pin. Pour into a mixing bowl. Melt the butter and stir into the biscuit (cookie) crumbs until well coated. Firmly press the biscuit (cookie) mixture into the base and up the sides of a 20 cm/8 inch springform tin (pan).

 2 Beat together the soft cheese and caster (superfine) sugar until well combined, then beat in the grated coconut and coconut-flavoured liqueur. Mash the 2 bananas and beat them in. Melt the dark chocolate and beat in until well combined.

3 Sprinkle the gelatine over the water in a heatproof bowl and leave to go spongy. Place over a pan of hot water and stir until dissolved. Stir into the chocolate mixture. Whisk the cream until just holding its shape and stir into the chocolate mixture. Spoon over the biscuit base and chill until set.

4 To serve, carefully transfer to a serving plate. Slice the banana, toss in the lemon juice and arrange around the edge of the cheesecake. Drizzle with melted chocolate and leave to set.

Rich Chocolate Ice Cream

A rich ice cream which is delicious on its own or with a chocolate sauce. For a special dessert, serve in these attractive trellis cups.

NUTRITIONAL INFORMATION

Calories 660   Sugars 56g
Protein .... 8g   Fat 46g
Carbohydrate ... 57g   Saturates 27g

40 MINS   0 MINS

SERVES 6

INGREDIENTS

ICE CREAM

1 egg

3 egg yolks

90 g/3 oz/6 tbsp caster (superfine) sugar

300 ml/½ pint/1¼ cups full cream milk

250 g/9 oz dark chocolate

300 ml/½ pint/1¼ cups double (heavy) cream

TRELLIS CUPS

100 g/3½ oz dark chocolate

3 Break the dark chocolate into small pieces and add to the hot custard. Stir until the chocolate has melted. Cover with a sheet of dampened baking parchment and leave to cool.

4 Whip the cream until just holding its shape, then fold into the cooled chocolate custard. Transfer to a freezer container and freeze for 1–2 hours until the mixture is frozen 2.5 cm/1 inch from the sides.

5 Scrape the ice cream into a chilled bowl and beat again until smooth. Re-freeze until firm.

6 To make the trellis cups, invert a muffin tray (pan) and cover 6 alternate mounds with cling film (plastic wrap). Melt the chocolate, place it in a paper piping bag and snip off the end.

7 Pipe a circle around the base of the mound, then pipe chocolate back and forth over it to form a trellis; carefully pipe a double thickness. Pipe around the base again. Chill until set, then lift from the tray (pan) and remove the cling film (plastic wrap). Serve the ice cream in the trellis cups.

1 Beat together the egg, egg yolks and caster (superfine) sugar in a mixing bowl until well combined. Heat the milk until almost boiling.

2 Gradually pour the hot milk on to the eggs, whisking as you do so. Place the bowl over a pan of gently simmering water and cook, stirring until the mixture thickens sufficiently to thinly coat the back of a wooden spoon.

Easy Chocolate Fudge

This is the easiest fudge to make – for a really rich flavour, use a good dark chocolate with a high cocoa content, ideally at least 70 per cent.

NUTRITIONAL INFORMATION

Calories 177   Sugars 21g
Protein .... 2g   Fat 10g
Carbohydrate ... 22g   Saturates 6g

 15 MINS   0 MINS

MAKES 25

I N G R E D I E N T S

500 g/1 lb 2 oz dark chocolate

75 g/2¾ oz/⅓ cup unsalted butter

400 g/14 oz can sweetened condensed milk

½ tsp vanilla flavouring (extract)

1 Lightly grease a 20 cm/8 inch square cake tin (pan).

2 Break the chocolate into pieces and place in a large saucepan with the butter and condensed milk.

3 Heat gently, stirring until the chocolate and butter melts and the mixture is smooth. Do not allow to boil.

4 Remove from the heat. Beat in the vanilla flavouring (extract), then beat the mixture for a few minutes until thickened. Pour it into the prepared tin (pan) and level the top.

5 Chill the mixture in the refrigerator until firm.

6 Tip the fudge out on to a chopping board and cut into squares to serve.

COOK'S TIP

For chocolate peanut fudge, replace 50 g/1½ oz/4 tbsp of the butter with crunchy peanut butter. Don't use milk chocolate to make this fudge as the results will be too sticky. Store the fudge in an airtight container in a cool, dry place for up to 1 month. Do not freeze.

Chocolate Liqueurs

These tasty chocolate cups are filled with a delicious liqueur-flavoured filling. They are a little fiddly to make but lots of fun!

NUTRITIONAL INFORMATION

Calories	 94	Sugars 8g
Protein	.... 1g	Fat 6g
Carbohydrate	.... 8g	Saturates 4g

30 MINS   0 MINS

MAKES 20

INGREDIENTS

100 g/3½ oz dark chocolate

about 5 glacé (candied) cherries, halved

about 10 hazelnuts or macadamia nuts

150 ml/¼ pint/⅔ cup double (heavy) cream

25 g/1 oz/2 tbsp icing (confectioners') sugar

4 tbsps liqueur

TO FINISH

50 g/1¾ oz dark chocolate, melted

a little white chocolate, melted or white chocolate curls (see page 57) or extra nuts and cherries

1 Line a baking tray (cookie sheet) with a sheet of baking parchment. Melt the chocolate and spoon it into 20 paper sweet (candy) cases, spreading up the sides with a small spoon or pastry brush. Place upside down on the prepared baking tray (cookie sheet) and leave to set.

2 Carefully peel away the paper cases. Place a cherry or nut in the base of each cup.

3 To make the filling, place the double (heavy) cream in a mixing bowl and sieve (strain) the icing (confectioners') sugar on top. Whisk the cream until it is just holding its shape, then whisk in the liqueur.

4 Place the cream in a piping bag fitted with a 1 cm/½ inch plain nozzle (tip) and pipe a little into each chocolate case. Leave to chill for 20 minutes.

5 To finish, spoon the melted dark chocolate over the cream to cover it and pipe the melted white chocolate on top, swirling it into the dark chocolate with a cocktail stick (toothpick). Leave to harden. Alternatively, cover the cream with the melted dark chocolate and decorate with white chocolate curls before setting. Or, place a small piece of nut or cherry on top of the cream and then cover with dark chocolate.

COOK'S TIP

Sweet (candy) cases can vary in size. Use the smallest you can find for this recipe.

Rocky Road Bites

Young children will love these chewy bites. You can vary the ingredients and use different nuts and dried fruit according to taste.

NUTRITIONAL INFORMATION

Calories	57	Sugars	6g
Protein	1g	Fat	3g
Carbohydrate	7g	Saturates	1g

 15 MINS   0 MINS

MAKES 18

I N G R E D I E N T S

125 g/4½ oz milk chocolate

50 g/2½ oz mini multi-coloured marshmallows

25 g/1 oz/¼ cup chopped walnuts

25 g/1 oz no-soak apricots, chopped

1 Line a baking tray (cookie sheet) with baking parchment and set aside.

2 Break the milk chocolate into small pieces and place in a large mixing bowl. Set the bowl over a pan of simmering water and stir until the chocolate has melted.

3 Stir in the marshmallows, walnuts and apricots and toss in the melted chocolate until well covered.

4 Place heaped teaspoons of the mixture on to the prepared baking tray (cookie sheet).

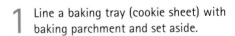

5 Leave the sweets (candies) to chill in the refrigerator until set.

6 Once set, carefully remove the sweets from the baking parchment.

7 The chewy bites can be placed in paper sweet (candy) cases to serve, if desired.

VARIATION

Light, fluffy marshmallows are available in white or pastel colours. If you cannot find mini marshmallows, use large ones and snip them into smaller pieces with kitchen scissors before mixing them into the melted chocolate in step 3.

Mini Chocolate Cones

These unusual cone-shaped chocolates make an interesting change from the more usual cup shape.

NUTRITIONAL INFORMATION

Calories 93   Sugars 7g
Protein . . . . 1g   Fat 7g
Carbohydrate . . . . 7g   Saturates 4g

🍰 35 MINS   🕐 0 MINS

SERVES 10

I N G R E D I E N T S

75 g/2¾ oz dark chocolate

100 ml/3½ fl oz/⅓ cup double (heavy) cream

15 g/½ oz/1 tbsp icing (confectioners') sugar

1 tbsp crème de menthe

chocolate coffee beans, to decorate (optional)

1 Cut ten 7.5 cm/3 inch circles of baking parchment. Shape each circle into a cone shape and secure with sticky tape.

2 Melt the chocolate. Using a small pastry brush or clean artists' brush, brush the inside of each cone with melted chocolate.

3 Brush a second layer of chocolate on the inside of the cones and leave to chill until set. Carefully peel away the paper.

4 Place the double (heavy) cream, icing (confectioners') sugar and crème de menthe in a mixing bowl and whip until just holding its shape. Place in a piping bag fitted with a star nozzle (tip) and pipe the mixture into the chocolate cones.

5 Decorate the cones with chocolate coffee beans (if using) and chill until required.

COOK'S TIP

The chocolate cones can be made in advance and kept in the refrigerator for up to 1 week. Do not fill them more than 2 hours before you are going to serve them.

Rum Truffles

Truffles are always popular. They make a fabulous gift or, served with coffee, they are a perfect end to a meal.

NUTRITIONAL INFORMATION

Calories 84	Sugars 9g
Protein 1g	Fat 5g
Carbohydrate . . . 10g	Saturates 3g

25 MINS   0 MINS

SERVES 20

I N G R E D I E N T S

125 g/5½ oz dark chocolate

small knob of butter

2 tbsp rum

50 g/1¾ oz desiccated (shredded) coconut

100 g/3½ oz cake crumbs

75 g/2¾ oz/6 tbsp icing (confectioners') sugar

2 tbsp cocoa powder

1 Break the chocolate into pieces and place in a bowl with the butter. Set the bowl over a pan of gently simmering water, stir until melted and combined.

2 Remove from the heat and beat in the rum. Stir in the desiccated (shredded) coconut, cake crumbs and 50 g/1³/4 oz of the icing (confectioners') sugar. Beat until combined. Add a little extra rum if the mixture is stiff.

3 Roll the mixture into small balls and place them on a sheet of baking parchment. Leave to chill until firm.

4 Sieve (strain) the remaining icing (confectioners') sugar on to a large plate. Sieve (strain) the cocoa powder on to another plate. Roll half of the truffles in the icing (confectioners') sugar until coated and roll the remaining truffles in the cocoa powder.

5 Place the truffles in paper sweet (candy) cases and leave to chill until required.

VARIATION

Make the truffles with white chocolate and replace the rum with coconut liqueur or milk, if you prefer. Roll them in cocoa powder or dip in melted milk chocolate.

Chocolate Marzipans

These delightful little morsels make the perfect gift, if you can resist eating them all yourself!

NUTRITIONAL INFORMATION

Calories	131	Sugars	19g
Protein	2g	Fat	6g
Carbohydrate	20g	Saturates	2g

 30 MINS   0 MINS

SERVES 30

INGREDIENTS

450 g/1 lb marzipan

25 g/1 oz/⅓ cup glacé (candied) cherries, chopped very finely

25 g/1 oz stem ginger, chopped very finely

50 g/1¾ oz no-soak dried apricots, chopped very finely

350 g/12 oz dark chocolate

25 g/1 oz white chocolate

icing (confectioners') sugar, to dust

2 Work the glacé (candied) cherries into one portion of the marzipan by kneading on a surface lightly dusted with icing (confectioners') sugar.

3 Do the same with the stem ginger and another portion of marzipan and then the apricots and the third portion of marzipan.

4 Form each flavoured portion of marzipan into small balls, keeping the different flavours separate.

5 Melt the dark chocolate. Dip one of each flavoured ball of marzipan into the chocolate by spiking each one with a cocktail stick (toothpick) or small skewer, allowing the excess chocolate to drip back into the bowl.

6 Carefully place the balls in clusters of the three flavours on the prepared baking tray (cookie sheet). Repeat with the remaining marzipan balls. Chill until set.

7 Melt the white chocolate and drizzle a little over the tops of each cluster of marzipan balls. Chill until hardened, then remove from the baking parchment and dust with sugar to serve.

1 Line a baking tray (cookie sheet) with a sheet of baking parchment. Divide the marzipan into 3 balls and knead each ball to soften it.

VARIATION

Coat the marzipan balls in white or milk chocolate and drizzle with dark chocolate, if you prefer.

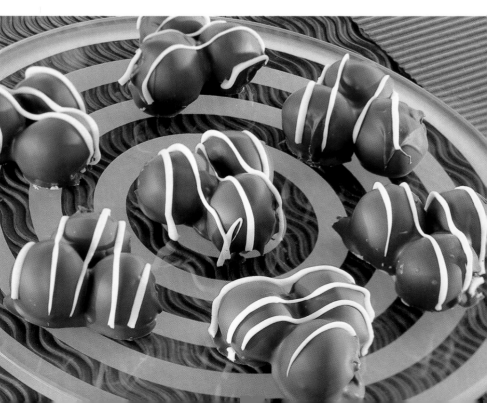

Chocolate & Mascarpone Cups

Mascarpone – the velvety smooth Italian cheese – makes a rich, creamy filling for these tasty chocolates.

NUTRITIONAL INFORMATION

Calories 75	Sugars 4g
Protein 1g	Fat 6g
Carbohydrate 4g	Saturates 4g

 25 MINS   0 MINS

SERVES 20

I N G R E D I E N T S

100 g/3½ oz dark chocolate

F I L L I N G

100 g/3½ oz milk or dark chocolate

¼ tsp vanilla flavouring (extract)

200 g/7 oz mascarpone cheese

cocoa powder, to dust

1 Line a baking tray (cookie sheet) with a sheet of baking parchment. Melt the chocolate and spoon it into 20 paper sweet (candy) cases, spreading up the sides with a small spoon or pastry brush. Place upside down on the prepared baking tray (cookie sheet) and leave to set.

2 When set, carefully peel away the paper cases.

VARIATION

Mascarpone is a rich Italian soft cheese made from fresh cream, so it has a high fat content. Its delicate flavour blends well with chocolate. You can use lightly whipped double (heavy) cream instead of the mascarpone cheese, if preferred.

3 To make the filling, melt the dark or milk chocolate. Place the mascarpone cheese in a bowl and beat in the vanilla flavouring (extract) and melted chocolate and beat until well combined. Leave the mixture to chill, beating occasionally until firm enough to pipe.

4 Place the mascarpone filling in a piping bag fitted with a star nozzle (tip) and pipe the mixture into the cups. Decorate with a dusting of cocoa powder.

Hot Chocolate Drinks

A hot chocolate drink in the evening can help you to ease away the stresses of the day. The nutritional information is for the spicy hot chocolate.

NUTRITIONAL INFORMATION

Calories 618   Sugars 48g
Protein . . . . 13g   Fat 43g
Carbohydrate . . . 48g   Saturates 26g

 10 MINS   0 MINS

SERVES 2

I N G R E D I E N T S

SPICY HOT CHOCOLATE

600 ml/1 pint/2½ cups milk

1 tsp ground mixed spice (allspice)

100 g/3½ oz dark chocolate

4 cinnamon sticks

100 ml/3½ fl oz/⅓ cup double (heavy) cream, lightly whipped

HOT CHOCOLATE & ORANGE TODDY

75 g/2½ oz orange-flavoured dark chocolate

600 ml/1 pint/2½ cups milk

3 tbsp rum

2 tbsp double (heavy) cream

grated nutmeg

1 To make Spicy Hot Chocolate, pour the milk into a small pan. Sprinkle in the mixed spice (allspice).

2 Break the dark chocolate into squares and add to the milk. Heat the mixture over a low heat until the milk is just boiling, stirring all the time to prevent the milk burning on the bottom of the pan.

3 Place 2 cinnamon sticks in 2 cups and pour in the spicy hot chocolate. Top with the whipped double (heavy) cream and serve.

4 To make Hot Chocolate & Orange Toddy, break the orange-flavoured dark chocolate into squares and place in a small saucepan with the milk. Heat over a low heat until just boiling, stirring constantly.

5 Remove the pan from the heat and stir in the rum. Pour into cups.

6 Pour the cream over the back of a spoon or swirl on to the top so that it sits on top of the hot chocolate. Sprinkle with grated nutmeg and serve at once.

COOK'S TIP

Using a cinnamon stick as a stirrer will give any hot chocolate drink a sweet, pungent flavour of cinnamon without overpowering the flavour of the chocolate.

Fruit & Nut Chocolate Fudge

Chocolate, nuts and dried fruit – the perfect combination – are all found in this simple-to-make fudge.

NUTRITIONAL INFORMATION

Calories 105	Sugars 21g	
Protein 1g	Fat 3g	
Carbohydrate ... 21g	Saturates 1g	

 15 MINS 0 MINS

SERVES 25

INGREDIENTS

250 g/9 oz dark chocolate

25 g/1 oz/2 tbsp butter

4 tbsp evaporated milk

450 g/1 lb/3 cups icing (confectioners') sugar, sieved (strained)

50 g/1¾ oz/½ cup roughly chopped hazelnuts

50 g/1¾ oz/⅓ cup sultanas (golden raisins)

1 Lightly grease a 20 cm/8 inch square cake tin (pan).

2 Break the chocolate into pieces and place it in a bowl with the butter and evaporated milk. Set the bowl over a pan of gently simmering water and stir until the chocolate and butter have melted and the ingredients are well combined.

3 Remove the bowl from the heat and gradually beat in the icing (confectioners') sugar. Stir the hazelnuts and sultanas (golden raisins) into the mixture. Press the fudge into the prepared tin (pan) and level the top. Chill until firm.

4 Tip the fudge out on to a chopping board and cut into squares. Place in paper sweet (candy) cases. Chill until required.

COOK'S TIP

Vary the nuts used in this recipe; try making the fudge with almonds, brazil nuts, walnuts or pecans.

This is a Parragon Book
This edition published in 2002

Parragon
Queen Street House
4 Queen Street
Bath BA1 1HE, UK

ISBN: 0-75257-535-X

Printed in China

NOTE

This book uses metric and imperial measurements. Follow the same units of measurement
throughout; do not mix metric and imperial. All spoon measurements are level: teaspoons
are assumed to be 5 ml and tablespoons are assumed to be 15 ml. Unless otherwise stated,
milk is assumed to be full fat, eggs are medium and pepper is freshly ground black pepper.

The nutritional information provided for each recipe is per serving or per person. Optional
ingredients, variations or serving suggestions have not been included in the calculations.
The times given for each recipe are an approximate guide only because the preparation
times may differ according to the techniques used by different people and
the cooking times may vary as a result of the type of oven used.

Recipes using raw or very lightly cooked eggs should be
avoided by infants, the elderly, pregnant women, convalescents
and anyone suffering from an illness.